Cinderella

by

P. H. Adams and Conrad Carter

SAMUEL FRENCH

FRENCH

LONDON
NEW YORK TORONTO SYDNEY HOLLYWOOD

PREFACE.

Of all our national forms of entertainment, the Pantomime is perhaps the most traditional and shows least signs of waning popularity. The average " run " of the professional pantomime is certainly as long as ever, and for many years it has been a source of considerable enjoyment and profit among amateur societies.

It is for this latter field of activity that this series of " BASIC PANTOMIME " has been specially designed, both as regards the " scripts," the settings, and the general production problems which face every company in work of this type.

Apart from the time-honoured stories on which all our pantomimes are (and rightly) based, much of their success depends on topicality, local and current humour, and by no means least upon the songs and choruses of the time—even of the year.

With this in view, these " basic " pantomimes have been prepared, not as the final, unalterable show, but as *bases* upon which may be built the ultimate product according to the desires, and the resources, of the individual company.

The scripts follow, in each case, the traditional stories very strictly. Any major departure would be resented by the youngest—and the oldest !—members of the audience. The dialogue is in modern prose, and prepared so that " cuts," additions, and the introduction of " local " or " topical " references may be effected with a minimum of difficulty.

Simplicity has been the prior aim also with regard to the settings, which are dealt with in detail in the " Production Notes " for each of the scripts. These contain suggestions for yet further simplification where the exigencies of the theatre are exceptionally limited, as well as indications of elaboration for those who are more fortunately placed.

Equal consideration has been given to the matter of Musical Numbers, Dances, etc. Those indicated represent what may be regarded as a reasonable minimum ; in fact, where resources are available, one or two extra numbers might be added with advantage. But the basic form which the pantomimes take render these additions quite easy to effect.

On the other hand, it will be found that, if desired, the pantomimes may be produced without alteration in any department despite the title of " BASIC " which has, for the foregoing reasons, been conferred upon them.

CINDERELLA

A PANTOMIME IN THREE ACTS

———

Characters:

BARON HANGOVER.

BARONESS HANGOVER.

HORTENSE.
ERMYNTRUDE. } The Baroness's ugly daughters.

CINDERELLA. The Baron's daughter.

BUTTONS.

THE FAIRY GODMOTHER.

THE PRINCE CHARMING.

Footmen. Men-at-Arms. Guests at the Ball.

Scenes:

MUSICAL NUMBERS:

Act I.

No. 1   *Opening Chorus* ...   . THE CHORUS

2   *Quartette,* " Baa, Baa, Black Sheep "
           BARON, BARONESS and SISTERS

3   *Duet*   ...   ... CINDERELLA and BUTTONS

4   *Song*   ...   . BARON

5   *Song*   ...   .   BUTTONS

6   *Song*   ...   .   CINDERELLA

7   *Duet*   ...   . The UGLY SISTERS

8   *Song* " Not For Me " ...   ... CINDERELLA

Act II.

9   *Opening Chorus* ...   . The CHORUS

10   *Song* " Who Knows " ...   PRINCE CHARMING

11   *Miming Scena*   ...   ... The COMPANY

11a   *Reprise of No.* 11
           FAIRY GODMOTHER and CHORUS

12   *Dance and Refrain*   ...   ... CHORUS
         (Prince and Cinderella dance only)

13   *Duet* " Single-hearted "
           PRINCE and CINDERELLA

14   *Duet*   ...   . The UGLY SISTERS

15   *Dance* (*Minuet*) ...   . PRINCIPALS

Act III.

16   *Song*   ...   . BARON

17   *Trio*   ...   ... BARONESS and the
           UGLY SISTERS

18   *Finale* " Cinderella ! "...   *Full Company*

PRODUCTION NOTES.

In many respects, "CINDERELLA" is the simplest of the three pantomimes published in this series. It may have, for some, a greater element of charm, probably because the romance of the neglected Cinderella and Prince Charming is the dominant feature of the play.

There is less "magic" and the effects are well within the capacity of a company having only the most modest resources.

The cast of principals is reasonably short, and there is ample scope for a small but efficient chorus.

SETTINGS:

These are devised on a similar basis to that of the other pantomimes—the use of cloths and wings rather than elaborate interior sets, which, however, can be resorted to if desired, and for which the published ground plans will be a considerable guide.

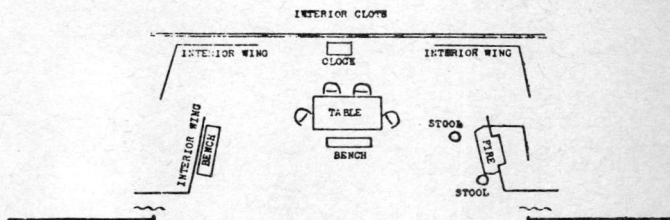

ACT I, Scene 1. This consists of a backcloth representing an interior, and a "book wing" down stage on either side with exits above them, suitably masked. These exits should be as wide as possible because, on the O.P. side, the doll's house and the sedan chair must be brought in. On the P.S. side, Cinderella makes her exit for a quick change and there must be space behind the P.S. book wing for her to do this. The furniture is of the simplest character.

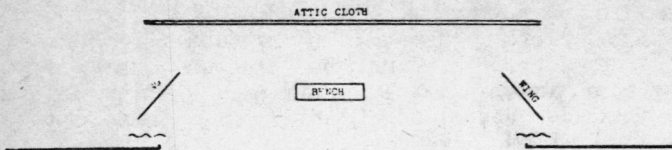

ATTIC CLOTH

BENCH

WING

Scene 2. This is the " attic " and consists solely of a cloth, and a small masking wing at either side. If necessary, a folding screen might be used, providing the curtain hides the sides of the stage sufficiently.

Scene 3. As for Scene 1.

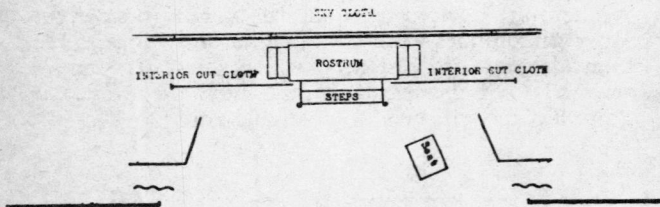

SKY CLOTH

INTERIOR CUT CLOTH   ROSTRUM   INTERIOR CUT CLOTH

STEPS

ACT II, Scene 1. An Ante-Room at the Palace. Here we have a plain sky-cloth (which may be retained throughout, the " kitchen cloth " being lowered in front of it) and a central rostrum and steps.

On either side of the steps an interior wing is run in, or (probably more conveniently) a cut cloth lowered to represent an interior with a wide central arch. Masking " book wings " are set down stage on either side.

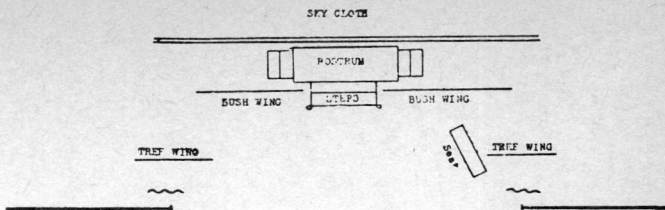

Scene 2. *The Palace Gardens.* The sky-cloth, rostrum, and steps remain set. The upstage wings (or cut-cloth) are replaced by low wings which represent, say, an ornamental shrubbery, or a stone balustrade with flowers backing it. One or two formal tree "cut-outs" would add to the garden effect. The down stage wings are single and should be painted to represent trees and foliage. Thus the change from Scene 1 to Scene 2 should be very quick indeed.

Scene 3. *The Ante-Room again.* There is, however, no reason why this scene should not be played in the garden if this is more convenient. This will avoid re-setting the Scene 1 cloths and wings.

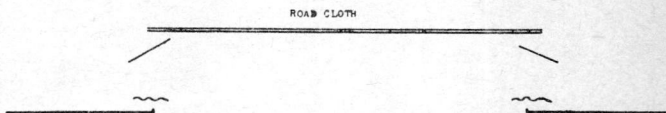

ACT III, Scene 1. This is merely a simple cloth, and can be painted as a street scene if desired. Or the scene may be played "in front of tabs."—a simple additional curtain leaving just enough "apron" for the few characters involved.

Scene 2. This is a return to the kitchen scene of Act I, Scene 1, and is precisely the same in every detail.

CINDERELLA

ACT I.

SCENE I.

SCENE.—*The Baron's Kitchen.*

> *Entrances R. and L. Table C., with chairs above and at each end, and bench below. Fireplace and stool L. See GROUND PLAN.*

The table is set out with breakfast things including porridge dishes. A pan of porridge is heating at the fire down L., which CINDERELLA tends as the Curtain rises.

(BEFORE *the curtain rises, the* CHORUS *is heard offstage singing, very softly, the refrain of some popular number, suitably chosen. Alternatively, the Curtain may rise on draw tabs and a chorus sing this refrain in front of tabs. They might be dressed, for instance, in long cloaks of various colours, with conical, " witches' " hats. If the tabs are plain, and a very pale colour, the only lighting might be a slow colour wheel, from perches. If the number is appropriate, each member of the chorus might hold a pocket torch— made to look like a candle—under his, or her chin.*)

No. 1. *Opening Chorus* ... ... CHORUS

(AFTER CHORUS: *Lighting fades to* BLACK OUT, *and* CURTAIN RISES. *The stage is in complete darkness. Then the lighting fades in very slowly—the glow of the fire first—to reveal* CINDERELLA *at the fireplace, tending the porridge. She is humming the last few bars of the refrain to herself softly. The lighting comes in to full, gradually. The clock strikes eight. The* BARON *hurries in R., to C. He gives a quick glance over his shoulder to R., and then moves to L.C.* CINDERELLA, *who has turned, moves to him.*)

CINDERS. Oh, good morning, daddy ! (*She puts her arms round him.*)

BARON. Good morning, my darling child !

(*He puts his arm round her and is about to kiss her when the BARONESS bursts in R. She stops short, arms akimbo and glares at him. His arm drops—he looks guilty and then sidles below the table and sits at the head R. end. The mother glares at CINDERS who is watching anxiously.*)

BARONESS (*roughly*). See to the porridge, girl. The minute my back's turned, you're fooling about with him. What do you think I keep you for . . . eating me out of house and home ? . . . I don't know why I put up with it. You mind your work, my girl, and I'll mind him.

(*During this she has moved to the table. She gestures BARON to foot of the table with thumb.*)

Out !

(*The BARON meekly crawls to the foot of the table L. end —while she takes the chair at the R. end. HORTENSE gushes on, R., and takes no notice of CINDERS, who says:*)

CINDERS. Good morning, sister.

(*HORTENSE goes to BARONESS and kisses her. CINDERS stirs the porridge.*)

HORTENSE. Good morning, mumsy.

BARONESS. Good morning, my dear.

(*HORTENSE goes to BARON, kisses him. He winces.*)

HORTENSE. Good morning, dadsy. (*Sits in R. chair above table.*)

BARON (*short*). Good morning.

(*ERMYNTRUDE enters slowly, yawning and rubbing eyes. She moves to R.C.*)

CINDERS. Good morning, sister.

(*ERMYNTRUDE grunts in reply, pecks at mother's cheek, says " Morning, mum," goes to BARON and starts to say morning but it develops into a prodigious yawn and she sits in L. chair above the table. She jostles other sister and they appear not to be on the best of terms.*)

BARONESS (*to CINDERS*). Serve the porridge, girl.
. . How much longer have we got to wait ?

(CINDERS *crosses with porridge above table to L.C.*)

HORTENSE (*who lisps throughout*). Weally, I don't know what skivvies . . . ah . . . ah . . . servants are coming to.

(ERMYNTRUDE *yawns rudely and* HORTENSE *glares at her.* CINDERS *serves the* BARON.)

HORTENSE (*snapping*). Serve the ladies first.

(CINDERS *moves to the* BARONESS.)

The manners of the lower classes are dreadful . . .

ERMYNTRUDE. You ought to know.

HORTENSE. And what do you mean by *that* remark ?

ERMYNTRUDE. What I says . . . you ought to know. You was one of 'em yourself last week.

(*During this,* CINDERELLA *serves porridge to them all, the* BARON *last, and then returns to the fire, L.*)

HORTENSE (*indignantly*). I never was . . .

ERMYNTRUDE (*calmly*). You was . . .

HORTENSE (*furiously*). Wasn't . . .

ERMYNTRUDE. *Was !*

HORTENSE (*snivelling*). Mumsy ! Hark at her . . . I wasn't, was I ?

BARONESS. Of course not. (*To* ERMYNTRUDE.) I'll have you know I've done my duty and brought you both up to be real ladies—(*Sniffs and wipes nose on back of hand*)—same as me.

HORTENSE (*tongue out at* ERMYNTRUDE). There ! You hear what Mumsy says !

ERMYNTRUDE (*unmoved*). Well . . . it's the first time as I knew you learned how to be a lady by selling winkles off a barrer down the Old Kent Road.

(*The* BARON *guffaws. The* BARONESS *turns angrily on him.*)

BARONESS. You've got nothing to snigger at . . . you're glad enough to live on the money we made selling winkles.

HORTENSE. Winkles, winkles . . . Oh, mumsy, do stop talking about winkles. . . .

BARONESS (*peeved*). Why should I ?

ERMYNTRUDE (*enjoying this*). Yes . . . why should
she ? I wish I'd got a nice plate of them now . . .
this porridge is burnt again.

BARONESS (*aghast*). What ! (*Tastes it.*)

HORTENSE. Not again ? (*Tastes it.*)

BARON. I think the porridge is very nice—very
nice indeed.

(BARONESS *and* HORTENSE *both slam spoons on the
     table.* ERMYNTRUDE *removes porridge from her eye.*)

BARONESS (*to* BARON). Bah !

HORTENSE (*to* BARON). Bah !

CINDERS (*up L.C. tearfully*). But I stirred it until
my arms ached. It *can't* be burnt !

HORTENSE. Bah !
                    (*Introduction to Song.*)

BARONESS. Bah !

ERMYNTRUDE. Bah !

No. 2.   QUARTETTE. " *Baa, Baa, Black Sheep.*"
     HORTENSE, ERMYNTRUDE, BARONESS, BARON

ERMYNTRUDE. (*Sings.*)
    Baa, baa, black sheep
    Such a row I've never heard
    'Cos Cinders burnt the porridge
    You're giving her the bird
    But now we're in the upper class
    You really must agree
    You shouldn't cuss the servants
    In High Society.

(ALL *except* CINDERS, *sing the last four lines again after
              each verse.*)

HORTENSE. (*Sings.*)
    Baa, baa, black sheep
    What a lot of utter tripe
    I'll cuss the servants when I please
    With language rich and ripe
    But I'll heed the rules of etiquette
    Respect my pedigree
    And always say " pardon " (*Hand on her chest.*)
    In High Society.
           (ALL: *Chorus last four lines.*)

BARONESS. (*Sings.*)
>   Baa, baa, black sheep
>   There's a lot in what you say
>   Forget your horrid past, me dears
>   Think what you are to-day
>   The nouveau riche, the upper ten
>   Of aristocracy
>   Don't drink out of your saucer
>   In High Society.
>   (ALL: *Chorus last four lines.*)

BARON. (*Sings.*)
>   Baa, baa, black sheep
>   Your precepts may be crude
>   Your bearing coarse, your accents vile
>   Your manners rough and rude
>   But please remember me, my dears
>   Respect the family tree
>   And don't bring shame upon my name
>   In High Society.
>   (ALL: *Chorus last four lines.*)

(BUTTONS *enters during last chorus. He has a letter with a large seal on back, in his hand. He shows it freely. He goes down L.C. to the* BARON *and bows.*)

BARON. Yes—er—er—Buttons?

BUTTONS. A letter, m'lord, from His Royal Highness, Prince Charming.

(*Exclamations from* BARONESS *and* DAUGHTERS. *The* BARON *holds out his hand for the letter but the women rise (except* CINDERS) *and clamour for the letter.* BUTTONS *holds it above his head.*)

HORTENSE (*excitedly running round R. of table*). From the Prince . . . give it to me . . . quick!

ERMYNTRUDE (*coming round L. of table*). No, no, give it to me!

(CINDERELLA *watches from her stool L.*)

BUTTONS. It's addressed to the master . . . I'll give it to him.

BARONESS. Buttons. . . . Hand me that there letter!

BUTTONS (*reluctantly*). It's for the master, m'lady!

BARONESS (*grimly, stalking down C., below table*). Well ?

BUTTONS (*embarrassed*). I—er—the master—the man—I mean the one (*Indicates* BARON) that wears the breeches, m'lady.

BARONESS (*more grimly*). Well ?

(BUTTONS, *with a shamefaced look at the* BARON, *moves down C., hands over the letter to the* BARONESS, *and crosses to R.C., dusting his hands elegantly. The daughters crowd round in excitement while the* BARONESS *relishes the thrill of opening a letter from a Prince. Then her cautious nature shows through.*)

(*Turning to* BUTTONS.) Here, you ! How do you know it's from the Prince . . . by his handwriting, I suppose ?

BUTTONS (*amused*). Handwriting . . . no ! He doesn't write his own letters . . . his secretary does that.

HORTENSE. His what ?

BUTTONS. His secretary.

HORTENSE. What's a sekertary ?

BUTTONS. He's the man who looks after the Prince's correspondence.

ERMYNTRUDE. Does what ?

BUTTONS. He writes the Prince's letters.

HORTENSE (*proudly*). Pooh ! I can write my own . . . and count up to twenty.

ERMYNTRUDE. Only in your bare feet.

BUTTONS (*exasperated*). So can he . . . but he's too busy . . . anyhow I know it's from the Prince because his seal's on the back.

BARONESS.
HORTENSE.   } (*Aghast*) His seal ?
ERMYNTRUDE.

BUTTONS. That's right . . . his seal.

HORTENSE (*blubbing*). Oh-h-h . . . the nasty man . . . someone has told him we used to be in the trade . . . and now he's insulting us by drawing fish on the back of our letter.

BARONESS (*crossing* ERMYNTRUDE *to* L.C., *to* BARON, *fiercely*). This is your doing . . . I know . . . laughing behind our faces . . . laughing in front of our backs . . . laughing at our behinds in front of our backs . . .

BARON (*rising hastily*). No, no, no, my dear, I assure . . . such an indelicacy would never occur to me. You are labouring under a misapprehension.

BARONESS (*nastily*). Oh no I ain't ! I ain't doing any more labouring any more . . . under Miss 'Appy Enshun or any of your posh friends. I'm Lady Hangover and I won't be insulted by any of 'em . . . Prince an' all.

BARON. But the Prince has not insulted you. The seal in question is not an aquatic creature but merely a waxen device for closing down or sealing a letter. The wax is stamped with the Prince's crest and is then known as a seal.

ERMYNTRUDE (*crossing* R.C. *below* HORTENSE, *to* BUTTONS). Why don't he lick his letters and stick 'em down ordinary ?

BUTTONS. Because he's not ordinary. He's a prince, and princes don't lick.

ERMYNTRUDE. Eh ? Don't lick ?

HORTENSE. No !

ERMYNTRUDE. Coo-*er* ! . . . I'll bet he has a job with a tuppenny cornet ! (*Laughs raucously.*)

HORTENSE. Oh, mumsy, do open the letter . . . I'm so excited—ever so !

ERMYNTRUDE. So'm I, so'm I !

(BARONESS *turns back to* C., *below table.*)

CINDERS. And I am too ! (*Comes to below* L. *end of table.*)

ERMYNTRUDE. What ! You ?

(BARON *coughs, embarrassed, moving* L.)

HORTENSE. Eh ? You ? What's the prince got to do with you . . . you're only a servant.

CINDERS (*stung*). Well . . . it's my daddy he's written to !

BARONESS. Hold your tongue and get the washing up done . . . and remember . . .

ERMYNTRUDE. Oh, don't bother about her. Open the letter and let's see what's in it.

(CINDERELLA *returns slowly to the fire.*)

BARONESS. Can't you wait a minute . . . (*She opens the letter and reads*) . . . Oh . . . oh-h . . . oh-h-h-h ! (*Ecstatically, rising.*) OH . . . OH-H-H . . . what do you think it is ?

BARON (*gloomily*). The electric light bill.

BARONESS (*triumphantly*). NO ! An invitation (*strikes a pose*) to the Palace ball tonight . . . for myself and my two daughters . . . and, of course,— you— (*Indicates* BARON.)

HORTENSE. Oh, read it out, Mumsy dear.

ERMYNTRUDE. Yes, go on. I want to hear what he's writ.

BARONESS. Very well. (*Reads.*) " H.R.H. Prince Charming commands the attendance of Lord and Lady Hangover and their daughters at a ball to be held at the Palace tonight at 9 o'clock."

CINDERS (*enthusiastically*). Then I'm invited too. (*Rushes to embrace* BARON.) Oh, daddy !

HORTENSE. Of course you're not invited . . . it isn't a servants' ball.

CINDERS (*stamps her foot angrily*). I AM invited ! (*Comes down L. C.*) It says Lord and Lady Hangover and their daughters . . . and I'M a real daughter . . . not a step-one.

BARONESS. Don't you insult your sisters by calling them step-ones . . . I've a good mind to whip you.

CINDERS. I don't care . . . it's true . . . they're not real daughters . . . and you're not a real wife . . . you're only second-hand !

(*The* BARON *and* BUTTONS *guffaw. The sisters are astounded, the* MOTHER *outraged and* CINDERS *a little frightened at her temerity.*)

BARONESS (*rushing at Cinders*).   You little . . . take that !

(*She swings back her arm to strike* CINDERS *and knocks* HORTENSE *back instead.* HORTENSE *steps heavily on* ERMYNTRUDE *who retaliates by smacking her head.* HORTENSE *howls and mother comforts her. The men and* CINDERS *enjoy it and* ERMYNTRUDE *hops round nursing her foot.* BUTTONS *dances delightedly round above the table to L.C.* CINDERS *runs to* BARON *L.*)

BARONESS. There, there then. Mumsy didn't mean to clout her precious little flower—(HORTENSE *howls*)—it's all that cheeky Cinders fault . . . (*Howl.*) . . . now dry your ickle peepers den or you'll spoil your face for the ball . . . (*Howl.*) . . . shush, shush, there's an angel, and we'll go and buy a new frock for tonight.

(*During this* BUTTONS *and* BARON *help* CINDERELLA *to clear the table.*)

ERMYNTRUDE (*hopping up*). What about me . . . what about me ?

BARONESS. Yes, and you too . . . we'll all have new frocks.

ERMYNTRUDE. With pink roses ? (*Moving R.*)

HORTENSE. And lace frills ? (*Moving R.C.*)

ERMYNTRUDE. And flounces with chinchilla trimmings an' all that . . . none of this new-fashioned plain things—they're not decent. We'll set our *own* fashions !

BARONESS (*to R.C.*) You'll have the best that money can buy . . . no skimping . . . no skimping . . . we'll show 'em. (*To* BARON, *who is up C.*) and you too,—I can't have you spoiling my daughters chances . . . by looking like a scarecrow . . . you'll have to have a new doublet and hose . . . and a new wig. You can't go as you are now . . . half-naked.

CINDERS (*on his L.*). Why do you allow her to be so rude to us, Daddy ?

BARONESS (*up R.C.*). I'll tell you why, snippet ! Because he knows which side your bread is buttered !

CINDERS. Buttered ! There's been nothing but margarine since you came and . . .

BARONESS (*angrily*). And there won't even be
that unless you learn to keep a civil tongue in your head
. . . first you think you ought to go to the ball and
now you want butter on your bread. . . . Well . . .
I know a mother's duties and although you'll still get
margarine. . . . I'll let you go to the ball !

CINDERS (*rapturously*). Oh, thank you . . . thank
you. (*Over to* BARON). Daddy, I'm coming with
you.

BARONESS. Not so fast, not so fast. You *can* come
to the ball . . . when you've done your work.

CINDERS. Oh !

BARONESS (*pleasantly*). Now, get on with the
washing up, scrub the floors, do the dusting, bake the
bread, do the washing, fetch the sticks in, clean the
windows, make the beds, wash the back stairs, polish the
hall and, when you've finished . . .

HORTENSE (*down R.C.*). I've got some stockings you
can mend.

BARONESS. And when you've finished . . .

ERMYNTRUDE (*down R.*). I've got some smalls that
want washing out.

BARONESS (*to* ERMYNTRUDE, HORTENSE *and* CINDERS).
AND when you've finished . . . you can come to the
ball.

(*She and the* DAUGHTERS *laugh uproariously.*)

CINDERS (*tears*). Oh, how cruel, how cruel !
(*To fireplace.*)

BARON (*sepulchrally*). Oh malice, malevolence . . .
malignity ! Oh . . .

BUTTONS (*up L.C.*). And what's she to do in her
spare time . . . fire watching ? (*Or topical gag.*)

BARONESS. You shut your . . . hold your tongue.
I'll see you have plenty to do . . . outside ! I don't
want you helping her . . . not that you're likely to
. . . you and work ain't good friends. (*Pleasantly
to others.*) And now that's settled, we'll go to town and
buy our dresses. Come along, daughters !

(BARONESS *stands aside as they exit and beckons to the*

BARON *who has hung back to speak to* CINDERS.)
Come along, *husband* !

(*Exits with* DAUGHTERS.)

(BARON *goes to comfort* CINDERS.)

BARONESS (*off stage*).   Egbert !

(BARON *groans and runs off R.*)

(CINDERS *goes and sits dejectedly on stool.* BUTTONS *waits a moment and then gesticulates angrily.*)

BUTTONS.   The fishy-faced old Jezebel !   That invitation is just as much for you as for the others. The slimy old toad . . . (*Comes down C., below the table.*)   You know why she won't let you go ?   Because she knows you'll spoil the chances of her two beautiful daughters. (*Pretends to read and mimics.*)   " The Honourable Miss Hortense Hangover and her charming sister the Honourable Miss Ermyntrude were the belles of the bell.   Though slightly cracked, I fear, they made a hollow noise when I tapped them . . ." (*Laughs.*) . . . Spoil their chances !   Why, with all their fine clothes, and their money they can't hold a candle to you. . . .   D'you know what it is ?   They're jealous of you, dear Cinders . . . just plain, downright jealous !

CINDERS (*coming downstage L. of* BUTTONS).   But it's no good . . . I shan't be able to go . . . I'll never finish all that . . .

BUTTONS.   Not by yourself . . . but with me to help you, you will.

CINDERS.   But stepmother said . . .

BUTTONS.   We aren't going to worry about what *she* said !   Come on, the sooner we start the sooner we finish.

CINDERS (*sits on bench below the table*).   Oh, Buttons, do you really think we can do all that work ?

BUTTONS.   Of course we can ; and when it's done, she'll *have* to let you go to the ball.

CINDERS.   She *said* she would . . . unless she gets angry and changes her mind.

BUTTONS.   Then we must see that she doesn't get angry. . . .   What *does* she get angry about ?

CINDERS.   Over most things . . . but usually over Daddy . . . or me.

BUTTONS.   Well, it's your job to see she doesn't get angry over you . . . but the baron . . . that's *my* job !

CINDERS.   Yes.   She was terribly angry with him yesterday.   If she catches him at it again, she'll be furious.   We shall have to stop him, Buttons—you'll have to stop him ; you'll have to get it away from him.

BUTTONS.   Yes, but how ?   (*Sits, R. of* CINDERELLA.)

CINDERS.   Oh, I don't-know.   Any way you can think of.   Borrow it, steal it, do anything ; but do get it away from him.

BUTTONS.   I'll do my best . . . yes . . . I think I can manage it.

CINDERS.   Oh, good old Buttons . . . (*She hugs him*) . . . and now let's get on with the work.   You do the sweeping and I'll do the scrubbing.

(*She goes to fetch a pail and scrubbing brush from down L., and* BUTTONS *fetches a broom from R.   As they work, they go into* DUET, *working all through the verses, which they share, and pausing in their work for the refrain.*)

No. 3.   *Duet*   ...   CINDERELLA *and* BUTTONS.

(*At end of Number* :—)

CURTAIN.

During scene change : CINDERELLA *and* BUTTONS *come down in front of tabs for 2nd Refrain* (*and dance if desired*).

Act I.

Scene 2.

Scene.—*The Baron's Attic.*

The Baron *is seated dejectedly on a bench.   He goes into:—*

No. 4.   *Song* ...   . Baron.

Baron.   O dear, O lor ! O lor, O dear ! What on earth made me marry that Awful woman ? And of all people, the widow of a Whelk Stall King ! Just because I was broke and she wanted to be a Lady ! Lady ! (*buries his head in his arms and moans ; then looks up.*) I did it all for my darling Cinderella—and now the poor little mite doesn't even get a Saturday ha'penny ! She's the apple of my eye—and look how she's tied to the kitchen. If I wash up, there's a row ! If I scrub a potato there's a hurricane ! If I wipe the sink there's an earthquake ! The only comfort I have now is my music—and even that I have to enjoy in secret. (*Brings trumpet out of his coat.*) I only played downstairs once—I've still got the bruises ! O misery me ! O lack-a-day ! What a *faux pas* ! What a fiasco ! What a flop ! (*Polishes trumpet on his sleeve.*) Ah, well, while Cinders is doing the morning work, I'll have a bit of practice—she says I need it, though personally I think I'm getting on nicely—(*Blows an excruciating note.*)—Now !

(*He starts to play* " Home, Sweet Home." *He plays the verse—very badly—and starts the chorus.* Buttons *enters L., sucking a lemon. The* Baron *does not see him at first, but at the third line he looks at him, and despite all his efforts he can no longer control the notes issuing from the trumpet. Finally he stops playing and turns to* Buttons.)

Baron.   What do you want, Stoneleigh ?

Buttons.   Sh . . . sh ! You mustn't call me that here !

BARON. Oh no, of course. Though why you think it worth while to masquerade in my house as a servant and call yourself " Buttons," I can't imagine.

BUTTONS (*sitting L. of* BARON). I'll make a clean breast of it. I'm in love with your daughter Cinderella.

(BARON *reacts*.)

. . . and if I'd tried to court her as Lord Stoneleigh, I'd never have got near her for those Gorgons you've got yourself mixed up with.

BARON (*rising, paces R.*). I trust you win her . . . and very quickly. (*Turns back to C.*) There's no happiness for her here . . . (*Testily.*) But do put away that lemon. It distresses me. I want to practice. (*Lifts his trumpet to his lips.*)

BUTTONS. Wait ! I thought I heard a noise.

BARON. What noise ? I heard nothing. (*Sits.*)

BUTTONS. Sshh . . . listen !

(*They both listen intently.*)

Can you hear anything ?

BARON. No. Nothing.

BUTTONS. Me neither. Isn't it damned quiet ?

(*The* BARON *is annoyed at the disturbance. He shifts a little R., away from* BUTTONS *and starts to play again.* BUTTONS *again listens carefully. He suddenly moves to* BARON *and puts his hand on* BARON'S *arm.*)

There, that's it. Did you hear it that time ?

BARON (*peeved*). No, I didn't. Please don't interrupt. I'm playing.

BUTTONS. Playing ? What with ?

BARON. This . . . (*Holds out trumpet.*) My piano.

BUTTONS (*contemptuously*). Oh that.

BARON (*stung*). Yes, this. A most noble instrument.

BUTTONS (*contemptuously*). Ah . . .

BARON (*nettled*) What do you mean . . . " ah " ?
. . . Can *you* play ?

BUTTONS. Yes, of course I can play.

BARON. Oh, you can, eh ? Well, what do **you** play ? Strings?

BUTTONS. No, no, no, no.

BARON. Any brass ?

BUTTONS. Not much.

BARON. Wood, lad ?

BUTTONS. If I could, lad.

BARON. Percussion, perchance ?

BUTTONS. No, too soft.

BARON (*exasperated*). Then what do you play ?

BUTTONS. Dice ! (*Takes out dice.*)

BARON (*deflated*). Dice ! Gambling !

BUTTONS (*in the professional " chase-the-lady "
style. Rattling dice*). Yes, sir, dice. Civilisation's
gift to the hard-up and the henpecked. Takes your
mind off your troubles and puts money in your pocket.
The thrill of a lifetime in one small wooden cube.
Come along, sir, how about a little flutter. . . .

BARON. But I've never played before. I should
lose all my money.

BUTTONS. Not you, sir. I'll show you how to play.
Easy as falling off a house. You'll do well, sir. Un-
lucky in love—!ucky at cards. . . . I'm not sure I
should risk playing with you—you're bound to win.

BARON (*pleased*). Do you think so ?

BUTTONS. Sure of it, sir. But then, I'm a sportsman, big-hearted and generous and I'm always willing
to take a chance . . . if you don't speculate, you
don't accumulate.

(*They squat on floor as he throws dice.*)

We'll just have a trial run to see you've got the hang
of it.

(*They call the numbers as they fall, etc.*)

Now you've got it all right. We'll play for small stakes
to start with and increase as we go on. All right, sir ?

BARON. Yes . . . I think I know how to play
now.

BUTTONS. Good . . . then off we go.

(*Business of game—calling numbers.*)

Your game. That's two bob I owe you. Here you
are. You're pretty good. Never seen anyone pick it
up so quickly before.

BARON (*delighted*). Really . . . yes, it seems quite easy to a man of my intellect. Shall we increase the stakes ?

BUTTONS. If you like . . . but I think you'd better take it easy for a bit.

(*Business.*)

BARON (*delighted*). I do declare, I've won again. Shall we increase ?

BUTTONS. You seem to know it too well already for my liking . . . but I can't resist a little flutter. We'll double. My chuck . . . (*Business*, BUTTONS *appears dazed.*) It's uncanny ; I don't know how you do it. I've finished.

BARON. But you can't finish just because you're losing—I thought you said you were a sportsman . . . just as it was getting interesting.

BUTTONS. Oh well, if you put it like that . . . your throw.

BARON. I'll double. (*Throws.*)

BUTTONS. I'll take you. (*Throws.*)

BARON. I'll double again . . . oh . . . I've no money left . . . what do I do now ?

BUTTONS. Stake some security . . . your watch or something like that.

BARON (*troubled*). But I haven't got a watch . . . I've got nothing . . . but my trumpet.

BUTTONS. That's no good . . . I couldn't raise anything on that.

BARON (*nettled*). Yes, you could. It's a very valuable instrument. I always get at least thirty shillings on it.

BUTTONS. Oh, all right, shove it on.

(*The* BARON *throws a four and a five.*)

BARON. Four and five. (*He counts aloud on his fingers.*)

BUTTONS. That's eight all together.

BARON. No, no. Let me count . . . (*He counts nine on his fingers.*) See . . . it's nine. (*He demonstrates to* BUTTONS *who reluctantly agrees.*) There you've got nine to beat.　Not a bad throw, sir,—not a bad throw.

> (BUTTONS *throws.　He gets a four*.)

(*Hopping about in excitement*.)　Four . . . four . . . (*Counts hurriedly on fingers*.) . . . you've got to throw a six to win.

> (BUTTONS *makes great preparations to throw*.)

BUTTONS.　Let me see . . . five to win . . . five to win.

BARON.　No, no.　Six . . . six . . .

> (BUTTONS *throws.　It is a five*.)

(*Overjoyed*.)　Five, five, five . . . I've won . . . I've won.

BUTTONS.　No, you haven't,—I have . . . four and five make ten . . . count them up.

(*The* BARON *counts aloud again . . . when he gets to five a bell off stage strikes six.* BUTTONS *counts the bell and makes ten*.)

BUTTONS (*picking up the trumpet*).　TEN !　Dashed hard luck, sir, dashed hard luck, but allow me to hand you . . .

BARON (*dazed*).　Wh-what . . . ?

BUTTONS.　A lemon !　(*Hands him the lemon*.)

BLACK OUT.

During Scene change:

(*In front of tabs* BUTTONS *goes into* :—

No. 5.　*Song* (" The Man who Broke the Bank " *or other suitable song*) BUTTONS.)

CHORUS GIRLS *enter R. and L. for refrain, dance, etc.*

ACT I.

SCENE 3.

SCENE.—*The Kitchen.*   NOTE.—*Table and bench is moved further upstage.*

(CINDERELLA *is seated at fire, L.   She goes into:—*
          No. 6.   Song ...   .   CINDERELLA)

(*After Number:—Enter* BUTTONS *with trumpet case under his arm.   He comes down below table R.C., and* CINDERELLA *crosses down to him.   They meet, C.*)

CINDERS.   Oh, Buttons, you've got it.   You clever old darling !   How did you do it ?

BUTTONS (*simpers a little*).   'Twas ever so easy. I got him dicing.

CINDERS.   You didn't !

BUTTONS.   I did !

CINDERS.   Fancy poor old daddy playing dice with you !

BUTTONS (*laughs*).   Well, you wanted the trumpet taken from him, didn't you ?

CINDERS.   Oh, it's all right, Buttons . . . but (*she laughs*).   I thought everyone knew about you and your dice.

BUTTONS.   Seems as if most of them do.   I have a job to make any money at all nowadays . . . unless I work for it.

CINDERS.   Never mind, you'll meet plenty of new servants at the ball tonight . . . if we get there.

BUTTONS.   Golly, yes . . . how much more have you got to do ?

CINDERS.   I'm on the last one now   (*Holds up stocking.*) . . . If you dust the kitchen, I shall have finished ; thanks to you, Buttons.

BUTTONS (*sentimentally*).   I'd do anything for you, Cinders.   You know that, don't you ?

CINDERS.   Go on, you silly boy, and finish the dusting.

(BUTTONS *gets the duster and pirouettes around the room, stopping to flick the furniture with the duster.*)

BUTTONS (*sings as he dances round*).
          Now we'll all go to the Ball
          Baron and Buttons and Cinders and all
          We'll all get dressed in our Sunday best
          To pay the Prince Charming a call !

(*He stops.   Laughing.   CINDERELLA giggles.*)

Not bad, is it ?   I like the dance . . . I'll do it
again . . .   (*Waving the duster.*)
                    (BARONESS *enters behind him.*)
(*Dances and sings*)
          This duster will do, I suppose
          To wipe your old stepmother's nose
(*As* CINDERS *makes frantic signs to him to stop.*)
          The silly old guy will get one in the eye
          If she fancies the Prince will propose . . .

(*Thinking* CINDERELLA *is applauding, he bows low, with
     his back to the* BARONESS *whom he has not seen.*)

BARONESS (*smacking his seat*). WHAT ! (*He turns
and backs away.*)   So you're going to wipe my nose,
are you ? (*Advances menacingly.*)   So I'm a silly old
guy, am I ? (*Smacks him.*)   You're going to the Ball
I suppose ? (*Smack.*)   Are you ! (*Smack.*)   You'll
be too sore to dance by the time I've finished with
you . . .
(BUTTONS *evades a blow and she stumbles.   He takes
     this chance, cocks a snook at the* BARONESS *and exits
     R.*)
(*The* BARONESS *recovers her balance and glares round.
     She beckons the timid* CINDERS *out of corner down L.*)
BARONESS (*menacingly*). Come here.

                    (CINDERELLA *does not move.*)
Come here !

(CINDERS *advances cautiously out of range of an
                    umbrella.*)
What was he doing here ?
     CINDERS. He was helping me dust.
     BARONESS. And helping you to poke fun at me.
Didn't I tell you he wasn't to come ?

CINDERS (*nervously*).   He wanted me to go to the ball . . . so he came to help me.

BARONESS.   HE wanted you to go to the ball . . . and what about *me* ?   Where do you think I want you to go ?

CINDERS.   I . . . I don't know . . .

BARONESS.   I'll tell you !   Up those stairs to your attic . . . and there you'll stay, without bite or sup, until tomorrow morning . . . I'll teach you to disobey me.

She swipes at CINDERS, *misses her and chases her off stage, L.   The two Ugly Sisters enter by the R. door carrying numerous parcels, hatboxes, etc.)*

HORTENSE.   What are you doing, mumsy ?   You look very angry.   (*Above table.*)

BARONESS (*L.C.*).   I am very angry.   Cinders and that Buttons have been poking fun at me . . . and they had a funny idea that they were going to the ball tonight.   The only dancing that Cinder-wench will do will be in her attic . . . with bread and water for refreshments.

ERMYN. (*Down R.C.*).   But we want her down here, mum, to help us on with our new dresses—we do reellee !

BARONESS.   Down here ?   You don't think you are going to dress down here, do you ?

HORTENSE.   Yes please, mumsy darling.   Our rooms upstairs are so small and cold.

BARONESS.   You can't change down here . . . it ain't done !

ERMYN.   Well, we shall only muck our new frocks up if we both try to dress upstairs.

(*They put the parcels, etc., on the table.*)

HORTENSE.   Yes, mumsy . . . and there isn't time for us to dress one at a time . . . and we mustn't be late.   I mean !   What would the Prince say ?

(*The* SISTERS *giggle.*)

BARONESS.   Oh, all right . . . but mind you pull them curtains to . . . you ain't giving a free show to any of them village lads.

HORTENSE. We'll be very careful, mumsy dear. (*Kisses her.*) And will you send that girl down *please* !

BARONESS. Oh, all right—allright—all*right* !
(*The* BARONESS *exits L. as:—*)

(*The two girls undo their parcels, etc. During the next few speeches they move around preening themselves, displaying the contents of the parcels.*)

ERMYN. I'll bet they've never seen such dresses as we'll wear tonight. I reckon our mum's done us proud. Look at this 'ere ! (*Displaying cloak.*)

HORTENSE. Yes, she has. It wouldn't half make them stuck up cats at the Grammar school stare to see that, wouldn't it ? (*Displays another cloak.*)

ERMYN. I'll bet they would an' all. Specially when they get a dekko at my black.

HORTENSE. And my green moiré with the prim little bow in fondant pink . . . isn't it elegant . . . (*Displays dress.*) . . . so refined and tasteful . . . just the thing for distinctive wear at palace functions.

ERMYN. Look at this (*holds up a · hat.*)—ain't it ducky ? I'll tickle the Prince's fancy in this all right.

HORTENSE (*horrified*). Ermyn*trude* ! Don't be common !

ERMYN. (*unabashed*). Oh, I always think a tasty bit of millinery puts the finishing touch to a bloke, when he's on the point so to speak.

(*Enter* CINDERELLA *L.*)

HORTENSE. Well . . . of course . . . oh, here's the girl. (*Changing her tone.*) Get us two mirrors and then stay and help us dress for the ball.

(CINDERELLA *fetches two mirrors from the mantelpiece. The mirrors are placed one at each end of table, the sisters sitting by them.* CINDERS *must busy herself continuously with hats, mirrors, etc., above the table C.*)

I'm going to try my hats first.

ERMYN. So'm I . . . how many have you got ? I've got six.

HORTENSE.   So've I.

(*They are busy with hats and mirrors posing and trying different angles.   It is treated very seriously.*)

ERMYN.   I don't think this suits me.

HORTENSE.   Oh, yes it does, Ermyntrude. . . . It's your face it doesn't suit . . . it's a little too old for it. Let me see how I look in it. . . .

(*They exchange hats.   The effect is very ridiculous.*)

ERMYN.   The girl said they were all the rage . . . H'mmm ! . . . I can quite understand what all the rage was about . . . no, sister, not your type I'm afraid.

HORTENSE.   I'm afraid not . . . of course the style of my hair makes it so awkward to get a hat to fit, cher know !

ERMYN.   You shouldn't change it so often.

HORTENSE.   But I've got the most marvellous hair-dresser.   He's got a shop in the arcade . . . and such soft brown eyes and a lovely silky moustache.

ERMYN. (*absently*).   Try rubbing it with pumice stone . . .

HORTENSE.   Rub what ?

ERMYN.   Your moustache.

HORTENSE.   It's not my moustache . . . it's the hairdresser's.

ERMYN.   Then don't rub it.

HORTENSE (*crossly*).   I don't rub it . . . I go to have my hair done.   He's ever so nice . . . he gives me a reduction . . .

ERMYN (*trying on another hat*).   What do you think of this ?

HORTENSE.   (*Same bus. with another hat, not listening.*)   Of course, it should have had a shampoo and a bleach before tonight.

ERMYN.   Ow naow !   It would spoil the fur !

HORTENSE.   Fur !   Really, Ermyntrude, there's no need to be insulting !   Fur indeed !

ERMYN.   Well, I've always called it fur and I'm not calling 'em anything else, even if we are in society.

HORTENSE.   What are you talking about ?

ERMYN. This hat, of course . . .

HORTENSE. I thought you meant my 'air—*h*air !

ERMYN. Do you think . . . well . . .

HORTENSE (*confidentially*). Ermyntrude . . . have you ever been in love ?

ERMYN. Love . . . well, look at me ! Love . . . Have I gone all starry-eyed and dreamy ?

HORTENSE. What's it like being in love ?

ERMYN. It's like . . . it's like—er—er . . . just like a flock of sparrers going up your backbone. (*To* CINDERELLA.) What are you laughin' at ? (*Slaps her.*)

HORTENSE. Will you do my hair for me, sister dear ?

ERMYN. What ? Me ? . . . No, I can't abide messing about with anybody else's hair.

HORTENSE. Oh, please, sister dear . . . I'll lend you my lucky pendant charm for the ball if you will.

ERMYN. Thank *you*, but I've got enough charm of my own. . . . I'm not going to do your hair. Encouraging you in laziness. And don't be daft. If you don't want to do it yourself, make Cinders do it.

HORTENSE. That's an idea ! (*To* CINDERELLA.) Come on, now—hurry !

CINDERS. I'm afraid I don't know anything about hairdressing.

HORTENSE. You wouldn't ! Then go back upstairs until I call you . . . I'm not having you pinching all the secrets of my hairdressing.

ERMYN. Yes, go on ! You'd pinch anything.

(CINDERS *exits.*)

(ERMYNTRUDE *is still busy with hats.*)

I do think this is a saucy model . . . perhaps a trifle demi-mondaine, don't you think . . . (*Giggles.*) Nights in Paris !

HORTENSE. Oh, you might help me with my hair.

ERMYN. I've got me own to do.

HORTENSE. What there is of it !

ERMYN. Eh ? What's that ?

HORTENSE. Nothing. You are a mean pig, our **Ermyntrude.** You know I always catch cold when

I do my hair myself. (*She takes off her wig disclosing her bald head . . . she combs and brushes the wig.*)

ERMYN. Well, I'm going to try my dress on now. I'm so glad I chose black . . . it's so fetching.

(THEY *commence undressing. The following lines during business.*)

HORTENSE. And I'm glad I've got moiré . . . it's such sentimental stuff besides I find it so good for my morale.

ERMYN. I find an old and mild or a nice glass of stout is the stuff for my morale . . . puts some stiffening in your backbone.

HORTENSE. I think it more respectable to let my corsets do that.

ERMYN. Corsets . . . that reminds me . . . I want that girl to do me up the back . . . (*She goes to the door L. and shouts:—*) Cinders !

HORTENSE. Thank goodness I don't have to go thro' that performance. Don't you wish you had a figure like mine ?

ERMYN. I've got all the figure I want !

HORTENSE. And a bit over !

ERMYN. You only got yours by licking vinegar off the empty winkle plates.

HORTENSE. Really, Ermyntrude ! (*She busies herself with putting on her dress.*)

ERMYN. (*putting on her dress*). This black lace does marvellous things for my skin and it makes me look slimmer than ever.

HORTENSE. Lace is all very well for some people, but give me moiré with that prim little bow in fondant pink.

THEY *come down R.C., and L.C., preening themselves.*

(THEY *go into:—*)

No. 7. *Duet (and Dance) ...* THE UGLY SISTERS.

(THEY *finish at C. below the table.*

After Number:—

Re-enter CINDERELLA, L. *She comes to L.C.*)

ERMYN. (*to* CINDERELLA). Well ? How do I look, girl ?

CINDERS (*stammering*). Oh, you look f-f—beautiful, sister.

HORTENSE. What about me ?

CINDERS. L-l-lovely ! (*Turns away L. to hide her smile*).

(*The* SISTERS *embrace each other and giggle. The* BARONESS *and* BARON *enter* R.)

HORTENSE { How do we look, mums ?
ERMYN.   { How do we look, mum ?
          (*The* SISTERS *back to L.C.*)

BARONESS (*to C.*). Stand away from me, daughters, and then I'll be able to tell . . . you look beautiful . . . very, very beautiful . . . (*To* BARON *sharply.*) don't they, Egbert ?

BARON. Oh yes, yes . . . excruciatingly so.

BARONESS. There ! Your papa says you're excruciating . . . that's what they call chivalrous . . . (*Sits on bench below the table C.*) . . . and now papa is going to teach you how to curtsey because you'll have to do that at the ball tonight to all the gentlemen and an especially good one for the prince. Go on, Egbert.

BARON (*to R.C.*). Well, daughters, when you are introduced to the gentlemen they will bow to you and you must curtsey in return. The gentleman bows thus (*He bows.*) and the lady curtsies so (*He attempts to curtsey, the* SISTERS *follow his movements faithfully— lumbago bus.*) I'm afraid I shall have to ask Cinderella to show you that. Cinderella, please show your sisters how to curtsey.

(CINDERELLA *trips to C. and curtsies beautifully. The* SISTERS *try it with varying results.*)

Now, when you are presented to the Prince, you must do a much deeper curtsey—Cinderella !

(CINDERELLA *does a very low curtsey and goes down R.*)
Now, one for the Prince, (*Bus.*) again, (*Bus.*) again . . . now an ordinary one . . . (*Bus.*) and another. . . . (*Bus.*)

BARONESS (*rising*).   That'll do for that . . . but see that you walk upright . . . like this . . . follow me . . . (*To* BARON.) . . . you, too.

(*They mince round the stage.*   BUTTONS *enters up* R.)

   BUTTONS.   The coach is waiting, m'lord.

   BARONESS.   Then go and h'open it !   I 'ope it's h'aired !

(*Exit* BUTTONS R.)

(*They all pick up cloaks, etc., and move to exit* R. BARONESS *turns at* R., *to* CINDERS *who is kissing* BARON.)

And thank your lucky stars I'm kind enough to let you stay down here . . . and mind you have something 'ot waiting for us when we get back.

(BARONESS *exits, followed by the* BARON, *and then the* SISTERS *who flounce their fans at her as they pass.*)

(CINDERS *moves to bench* C., *crying quietly. She goes into* :—)

No. 8.   *Song* .. "Not for me" ... CINDERELLA.

(*The following lyric may be set to music or another number substituted.*)

   CINDERS.   (*Sings.*)
         Birds have nests amid the trees
         Ships find rest from angry seas.
         Where'er you roam, there's always home
            But not for me.
         The bells resound with clanging mirth
         Delight abounds on jocund earth
         There's untold joy for girl and boy
            But not for me.
               (*Rises, coming down* R.)
         Mighty river, babbling streams
         Flowing whither in my dreams ?
         To golden sands, and fairy lands
            I may not see   (*Moves to* L.C.)
         Restless the night with lover's sighs
         Soft the starlight in their eyes
         But earthly bliss so sweet as this
            Is not for me.   (*Moving* L..)

(BUTTONS *enters R.* CINDERS *is still crying.*)

BUTTONS (*moving down below table*).   Here, here !
Cheer up, Cinders !   You don't want to go to the rotten
old ball.   And I'd much sooner be here with you than
at the ball with dozens of other people.   We'll have
much more fun by ourselves.

CINDERS (*coming to him at L.C.*).   But I did want to
go to the ball and see the Prince.   He's so handsome.
. . .   Look, I've got a picture of him . . .   (*She
produces picture and sighs over it.*)

BUTTONS.   I think I'm as good looking as he is,
don't you ?

CINDERS.   Well, not quite, Buttons dear.

BUTTONS (*crestfallen*).   Well, I'll bet he can't do
Donald Duck.   (*He does Donald Duck from C., to R.C.*)

CINDERS (*smiling*).   I'm sure he couldn't . . . but
that doesn't really matter.

BUTTONS (*returning to C.*).   Cinders ?

CINDERS.   Yes, Buttons ?

BUTTONS.   Do you like me ?

CINDERS.   Of course I do.

BUTTONS.   Much ?

CINDERS.   Why yes, of course.

BUTTONS.   How much ?

CINDERS.   Oh—er—as much as I'd love a brother.

BUTTONS (*disappointed*).   Oh . . . are you in love
with the Prince ?

CINDERS.   Yes, I—I think so—and I did want to
see him.   (*Tears.*)

BUTTONS.   Never mind.   (*Pats her shoulder.*). . . .
Look . . . I'll go and fetch the doll's house and we'll
play with that.   I was cleaning it out yesterday. . . .
It's only just outside . . . wait a minute . . .

(BUTTONS *goes out R. and brings in the doll's house.*)

(*R.C.*)   Where shall we have it ?   Here ? . . . or
over there . . . by the fire ?

CINDERELLA.   No, no !   Up here—by the light.
(*She slips the bench under the table, and they bring the
doll's house up C.*)

What fun ! It's so long since we played with it . . .
(*She opens the front of the doll's house.*) . . . Oh !
You've forgotten the furniture !

BUTTONS. So I have ! I know where it is—I shan't
be a minute—

(*He runs out R.* CINDERELLA, *shutting the front of the
house, runs after him to R.C. calling* " Oh ! *and
Buttons . . .*" *There is a tapping inside the house.*
CINDERELLA *checks and turns at R.C. A voice inside
the house calls* " Cinderella ! Cinderella ! " CIN-
DERELLA *goes on tip-toe back to the house. There is
more tapping inside it, and the voice calls again*
" Cinderella ! " *She is just going to open the house
again, when the front flies open and the* FAIRY GOD-
MOTHER *comes out.* (*See lighting plot.*)

CINDERS (*darting back*). Oh !

F. GODMOTHER. Well ? Well, Cinderella ? Aren't
you glad to see me ?

CINDERS. Y—yes, of course I am—but who are
you, please ?

F. GODMO. I am your Fairy Godmother.

CINDERS. My—Fairy—*Godmother* ? I didn't know
I had one !

F. GODMO. Are you glad ? Eh ? Eh ?

CINDERS. Oh, of *course* !

F. GODMO. Good ! I notice you don't ask me
if I'm quite well today—well, I am quite well to-day,
but you aren't—Oh dear no ! You've been crying—
haven't you ? Haven't you ? What's the matter ?

CINDERS. N—nothing, Fairy Godmother. (*Crosses
GODMOTHER to L.C.*)

F. GODMO. Don't try to tell me fibs, Cinderella.
You ought to know better than to tell fibs to a godmother—certainly to a Fairy Godmother. I think
I can guess ! Have that horrid stepmother and ugly
step-sisters been ill-treating you—eh ? Eh ?

CINDERS (*nearly in tears*). Th—they wouldn't let
me go to the Palace to the Prince's Ball, and I *was*
invited . . . the invitation *said* . . . " and daughters."
(*She moves L.*)

F. GODMO. (*chuckling*). Wouldn't let ye go, eh ?
Why ? Don't tell me—I know ! Too pretty for 'em,
eh ? Put their noses out of joint, eh ? . . . Speak up,
girl, speak up !

CINDERS. I—I don't know, godmother.

F. GODMO. Rubbish ! Of course ye do ! Never
met a girl yet who didn't think she was prettier than
the rest—but in your case it's true. (*Chuckles.*) Any-
way—you're going—to—the *Ball* !

CINDERS. Me ? Going ? But I can't ! If stepmother saw me there she'd beat me . . .

F. GODMO. Yes, yes, yes—but she *won't* see you !
She won't even know who you are when I've finished
dressing you !

CINDERS. Are you going to dress me ?

F. GODMO. I certainly am !

CINDERS (*dancing with excitement*). N—not—not
in fairy clothes ?

F. GODMO. In fairy clothes . . . and a fairy
coach with two men to carry you to the Ball . . . and
you shall dance with the Prince . . . and be the envy
of every girl there, and all the rest of it . . . I know !
You might not think it, but I was young once myself !
(*Pats* CINDERS' *cheek.*) There, there ! But listen !
Your dress—your stockings—your fan—your lovely
glass slippers will be no use to you after the clock
has struck twelve ! Twelve ! You must be back by
twelve, *here* ! So see that you're back, or you'll find
yourself dancing with the Prince in the rags you're
wearing now ! Remember ! Back here by twelve !

CINDERS. Back here by twelve—very well—I
promise.

F. GODMO. Good girl—good girl ! Now to business
. . . (*Looks round.*) dear, dear ! There's nothing much
here to make a coach and footmen out of ! I shall
want a pumpkin ! A pumpkin—and some rats—or
mice !

CINDERS. Pumpkin ? Rats or mice ?

(BUTTONS *re-enters* R. *unseen by them.*)

F. GODMO. Bless the girl ! You don't expect me to make footmen and coaches out of thin air, do ye ?

CINDERS. N—no—I don't know . . . (Sees BUTTONS.) Oh, Buttons . . .

BUTTONS. I can't find the furniture anywhere . . . (Sees FAIRY GODMOTHER.) Oh, I beg your pardon— I didn't see the lady.

CINDERS. It's my Fairy Godmother. I'm going to the Ball !

BUTTONS (with a courtly bow). At your service, dear lady.

F. GODMO. I'm glad to hear it—(Chuckles, and whispers to him.) glad to hear it, Lord Stoneleigh ! (Digs him in the ribs, then raising her voice.) Instead of bowing and scraping, my man, get me a pumpkin, and some mice—or a rat or two !

BUTTONS. Cinders going to the Ball—pumpkins— rats—mice ! It doesn't make sense. . . .

F. GODMO. Go and get 'em, and stop gibbering . . . go on . . . be off !
(BUTTONS runs off R.)

CINDERS. Oh, I'm so excited ! You are a darling Fairy Godmother !

F. GODMO. (chuckling). Don't be ridiculous, don't be absurd . . .
(As BUTTONS enters with props.)
. . . ah, here he is ! Now to dress you—up you go to the fire where it's warm !
(CINDERELLA backs to the fire, wonderingly, as FAIRY GODMOTHER turns to BUTTONS.)
Put 'em down there—and off you go !

BUTTONS. Off ?

F. GODMO. Yes—off ! Unless you want to be turned into a toad !

BUTTONS. Br-r-r-r-r— !
(Runs off R.)

F. GODMO. (raising her arms, as the lights fade). Close your eyes, Cinderella ! Close your eyes !
(BLACK OUT.)
(Exit CINDERELLA for quick change.)

F. GODMO. (*chanting slowly in the darkness*)
    Fall the rags—and change to silk,
    Smooth and fine and white as milk.
    Shoes of glass, and jewels rare
    To adorn her arms and hair.
    Pumpkin vanish !—coach appear !
    In the place of mice draw near
    Footmen, at my fairy call
    Take this lady—to the BALL !

(*Immediately on the word " BALL " the lights go up. A sedan chair is at C., with two gorgeously liveried footmen. CINDERELLA is standing L.C., dressed very beautifully in her ball dress, but in her stockinged feet.*)

CINDERS. Oh, godmother, it's beautiful. . . . I've never seen so lovely a dress before. Oh . . . I'd thank you a thousand times but that wouldn't be enough.

F. GODMO. Chut, girl, be quiet. I'm your god-mother and that's enough for me.

CINDERS. Oh, it's lovely, lovely. (*She looks down.*) Oh, but I haven't any shoes.

F. GODMO. Tut . . . tut . . . I'd quite forgotten them. . . . Here they are. (*Produces glass slippers from dress. Chuckles.*) I made 'em out of the mouse traps !

CINDERS. Oh . . . Oh . . . glass slippers ! (*She slips them on.*) I shall be the most beautiful girl at the ball.

F. GODMO. There, what did I tell you. Vanity ! Vanity !

CINDERS. I want Buttons to see me !

F. GODMO. Yes, but hurry. You haven't much time.

CINDERS. Buttons ! Buttons !

        (BUTTONS *enters R.*)

BUTTONS (*rubs his eyes*). Christopher Columbus ! Cinders . . . I . . . I crave your pardon . . . The Hon. Miss Cinderella !

        (*He bows. She curtseys.*)

F. GODMO. Come along, child !

(FOOTMEN *open door of the sedan chair.*)

You can do all that at the ball. In you get and off you go and . . . enjoy yourself but . . . remember . . . twelve o'clock.

(CINDERELLA *crosses to the sedan chair. As she is entering, she turns to the* FAIRY GODMOTHER *and* BUTTONS.)

CINDERS. Good-bye, darling Godmother ! A thousand thanks ! Good-bye, dear Buttons ! (*She enters sedan chair.*)

(BUTTONS *and* FAIRY GODMOTHER *waving as the chair is carried off R.*)

BUTTONS. }
F. GODMO. } Good-bye ! Good-bye !

BUTTONS. I wish I was going.

F. GODMO. You are, Lord Stoneleigh . . . you *are* going to the Ball ! . . . You can't fool me . . . but you haven't a chance. She's in love with the Prince.

BUTTONS (*sighs*). I know, but I'd like to see her dancing, even with him. Did you say I was going ?

F. GODMO. I did. You're going—*now* !

BUTTONS. But how ?

F. GODMO. On the back of my broomstick. . . .

(BLACK OUT. FLASH . . . *thunder and wind*. BLACK OUT.)

CURTAIN.

END OF ACT I.

ACT II.

SCENE 1.

SCENE.—*An Ante-Room of the Palace Ballroom.*

(*When the Curtain Rises, the* CHORUS *is on the stage
and they go into:—*)

No. 9.   *Opening Chorus* ...   ...   CHORUS.

(*This should not be a waltz number.   It is suggested it
might be one with a tango rhythm, as a waltz number
opens a subsequent scene.*)

(*Towards the end of the Number, the* CHORUS *dance off
and the* PRINCE *and* BUTTONS *appear up C., on the
rostrum.   They are, of course, in Court dress.   The*
PRINCE *comes down the steps as he speaks,* BUTTONS
following, on his R.)

PRINCE.   I am glad you were able to come, Richard.
You are the only honest fellow at Court.

BUTTONS (*bows*).   I thank your Royal Highness.

PRINCE.   Have all the guests arrived ?

BUTTONS.   The Hangovers are still on the road.

PRINCE.   Ah, the Hangovers . . . an excellent old
gentleman, Hangover . . . Who is with him ?

BUTTONS.   His recently acquired second wife and
two step-daughters.

PRINCE.   Are they beautiful ?

BUTTONS.   Ugly, sir.

PRINCE.   Ugly ?

BUTTONS.   As sin, sir.

PRINCE.   Ah . . . money, I suppose ?

BUTTONS.   Yes, sir.   Ch'rm !   (*Waves his lace
handkerchief delicately.*)   Fish, I believe !

PRINCE.   Good heavens !   Poor Hangover ! . . .
I just remember his first wife . . . a beautiful and
charming lady . . . a pity he hadn't a daughter like
her . . . a pity, eh, Buttons ?

BUTTONS.   But, Your Highness, he . . . (*Checks
himself.*)

PRINCE.   Yes ?

BUTTONS.   Oh, nothing, sir—nothing.

PRINCE (*sighs*).   Ah. well. . . .   Go, Richard, and see if there is news of them.   When they arrive you will receive them in here . . . I will appear later.

BUTTONS (*bows*).   As your Royal Highness commands.

(BUTTONS *exits R.*)

(*The* PRINCE *picks up a lute and striking a few chords, sings:—*)

No. 10.   *Song* " Who Knows ? "   PRINCE.

PRINCE.   Who knows a green and pleasant field
Where butter-cups their golden pollen yield
Who knows of singing birds and shady lanes
Where Love is King—and sweet contentment reigns.
Oh, knew I then such blithe tranquillity
There would I live and love—in Arcady.

Verse 2.

Who knows a sweet and pleasant maid
With tender eyes that twinkle unafraid
With shining hair and Cupid's crimson bow
With all the charm that Nature can bestow
Would that I knew such a one as she
To be my bride—to share my Arcady.

(BUTTONS *re-enters R.*)

BUTTONS.   Your Highness, the Hangovers will be here shortly.

PRINCE.   Ah, yes, Richard. (*Sighs.*)   The same simpering, snivelling lot . . . full of flattery, conceit and coquetry . . . I am sick to death of it.

BUTTONS.   Courage, sire.   It won't last so very long and . . . who knows . . . there may be someone here tonight who is different . . . even . . . interesting.

PRINCE (*drily amused*). Don't tell me they're bring-
ing a troupe of performing fleas, Richard. (*He moves
to door.*) I shall return when you've got them on the
jump.

(PRINCE *exits L., after acknowledging* BUTTONS' *bow.*)

BUTTONS. There'll be more things jumping tonight than fleas, my master. Hold fast to your heart-
strings when you see my Lady Cinderella or you'll
lose it more quickly than Hangover lost his trumpet.
(*Turns to door R.*) What ho there, fellow !

(FOOTMAN *enters, R.*)

FOOTMAN. M'lord ?

BUTTONS. Show the circus in here when it arrives.

FOOTMAN. The . . . the circus, m'lord ?

BUTTONS. Yes, yes, the circus—the aristocracy—
the nobility—the blue-bloods—the Hangovers—show
'em in here.

FOOTMAN. Very good, m'lord.

(*Exits.*)

BUTTONS. Now for it ! (*Goes to down L.C.*)

(*A bell rings and the* FOOTMAN *re-enters R.*)

FOOTMAN (*announcing R.C.*). My Lord and Lady
Hangover and their daughters the Honourable Misses
Hortense and Ermyntrude Hangover.

(*The* BARON, BARONESS *and* SISTERS *enter R. The
    SISTERS curtsey to the* FOOTMAN ; *the* BARONESS *sees
    them and gives one a push that wrecks the curtsey,
    and comes C.*)

BUTTONS (*bows to* BARONESS *and* BARON). Your
servant, milady . . . milord . . .

(*The* SISTERS *whisper aside, down R., as* BARONESS
            curtsies, BARON *bows, etc.*)

HORTENSE. It's the Prince.

ERMYN. Ooohh ! . . . ain't he lovely . . . look
at his hair . . . and his legs !

HORTENSE. What shall we do ? Do we have to
curtsey ?

ERMYN. I don't know . . . I've forgo . . let's
ask him.

(THEY *make tentative approaches to* FOOTMAN *who remains aloof and scares them off, by throwing up his chin, turning R. and going off.*)

HORTENSE. I don't like him.

ERMYN. Ain't he stuck up ?

(*The* BARON *indicates his daughters to* BUTTONS *who approaches them.*)

Look out . . . he's after us.

HORTENSE. Oh dear, oh dear, what shall we do ?

(BUTTONS *bows, they goggle at him, huddled together.*)

BUTTONS. Ladies, your servant.

BARONESS (*hisses*). Curtsey, you fools, curtsey.

HORTENSE (*pushing* ERMYNTRUDE). Curtsey, you fool, curtsey.

(THEY *curtsey.* ERMYNTRUDE *trips and staggers forward.*)

BARON. Daughters . . . this is Lord Stoneleigh.

HORTENSE. I thought he was the Prince.

ERMYN. (*slapping* BUTTONS *on the back*). Well, chase me Aunt Fanny, I thought you was the Prince !

BUTTONS. Oh no ! The Prince will be here soon. . . .

(*Fanfare off.*)

Ah, there he is now.

(ERMYNTRUDE *scurries back to* HORTENSE *at R.,* BARON *and* BARONESS *are at L.C.* BUTTONS *moves up C. Enter two men-at-arms. The* SISTERS *are agog with excitement.*)

HORTENSE (*to* ERMYNTRUDE). Who are they ?

(*The men-at-arms stand R. and L. of the steps.*)

ERMYN. Boy Scouts !

(*Enter the* PRINCE *C. The guests curtsey or bow as he comes down to C.*)

BUTTONS (*L. of* PRINCE). May I present, your Royal Highness, The Lord and Lady Hangover.

(*The* PRINCE *bows to them.*)

And their daughters, the Honourable Miss Hortense (*Curtsey.*) — the Honourable Miss Ermyntrude. (*Curtsey.*)

(*The* PRINCE *is a little staggered. then bows coldly.*)

PRINCE. I trust you will enjoy the ball, ladies.
(THEY *try to speak but the words do not come, so they
                      giggle*.)
. . . Are you fond of dancing ?
(*The* FAIRY GODMOTHER *enters L. and* BUTTONS *bows.
                  to her*.)

HORTENSE (*simpers*). Oh yes, your Royal Highness,
I simply adore it. I'd die if I couldn't dance, I think
it's too, too definiteleh divain . . . definiteleh !

PRINCE. Ah, yes, of course . . . (*To* ERMYN-
TRUDE.)—and you, madam ?

ERMYN. Don't bother to call me madam, your
worship, call me Ermy . . . all me friends do.

PRINCE (*coldly*). Er—I thank you.

ERMYN. And I'll call you Princey, eh ? . . . Your
worship sounds too much like the petty sessions.

BARONESS. Answer the Prince's question, Ermyntrude, he said did you like dancing ?

ERMYN. I 'eard ! . . . coo . . . not 'arf. . . .
You should see me rumba. . . . I like the rumba
. . . gives you plenty of chance to waggle. . . .
Do you waggle, Princey ?

PRINCE. I'm afraid not, but . . .

HORTENSE (*interrupts*). I prefer the stately, re-
fained measures. I think they're too, too divaine . . .
definiteleh ! It gives one the opportunity of making a
leg.

ERMYN. Oohh . . . I think the Princey's legs are
lovely, don't you . . . ? . . . Better'n his'n . .
(*Indicates* BUTTONS.)

HORTENSE. Yes, and mine are, too. (*Lifts her
skirts*.) Do you like my legs, Prince ?

PRINCE (*fed up*). Madam, I am a vegetarian. (*Turns
C. to talk to* BUTTONS.)
              (*Dance music from off stage*.)

HORTENSE. ⎱ The band !
ERMYN.   ⎰ Can we dance, mum ?

BARONESS (*scolding*). No. You must wait for the
Prince. (*All in one word*.) Whatever-next-I-never-
did !

ERMYN. Who's he going to dance with, mum ?
HORTENSE. Me, I hope. (*Approaches* PRINCE *but
the* BARONESS *detains her with a gesture, coming to* C.)
BARONESS. Not so fast. After your elders, girl.

No. 11.   *Miming Scene* ...   ... PRINCIPALS.

(*The following is pure mime, set to music. There is no
dialogue or singing*:)

The BARONESS *dances up to the* PRINCE, *who turns
away. She dances back.*

The SISTERS *each dance up to the* PRINCE, *and are
in turn rejected.*

The FAIRY GODMOTHER *dances to the* PRINCE, *and
he bows to her. She waves her arm towards the steps
and the* PRINCE *turns to look up* C.

CINDERELLA *is standing on the rostrum up* C.

The PRINCE *is overwhelmed by her beauty, and
holds out his hand.* CINDERELLA *comes down, takes
his hand, and they waltz off, leaving the others
amazed.*

The FAIRY GODMOTHER *then dances off with*
BUTTONS, *the* BARON *seizes the* BARONESS *and dances
off with her.*

The SISTERS *both approach the* MEN-AT-ARMS, *who
tilt up their chins, about turn and march off. Disgusted, the two* SISTERS *swing round to* C., *and collide
violently. Then, very bad tempered, they dance off
together.*

CURTAIN.

During Scene change:—

In front of tabs:—FAIRY GODMOTHER *with Ladies
of the Chorus enter and go into*:—

No. 11a.   *Reprise of Miming Number*
FAIRY GODMOTHER AND CHORUS.

(GODMOTHER *sings verse of the Number used for the*
MIME, *with refrain by* CHORUS.)

Act II.

Scene 2.

Scene.—*The Palace Gardens.*

No. 12.   *Dance and Refrain*   ...   Chorus.

(*The* Chorus *dance on R., singing if desired. Among the couples are the* Prince *and* Cinderella. *This Number should be a waltz refrain. The* Chorus, *as the Number ends, dance off R. and L., leaving the* Prince *and* Cinderella *at C. They stop dancing as the music dies, but remain in each other's arms.*)

Prince. I have never known anyone dance so beautifully.

Cinders. Thank you. I could dance for ever with you, my Prince.

Prince. *Thank* you, my lady. (*He holds her at arms length.*) You are like your dancing, without flaw, perfect . . . beautiful.

(Cinders *is bashful.*)

Why have I never seen you before? I have searched my realm for you—far and near—where have you been hiding?

(Cinderella *moves to L.C.*)

Cinders. Then you did not search well enough, sire. I have been hiding not a hundred miles away from here.

Prince. What is your name, my beautiful one? And why have I never heard of you?

Cinders. It is a name you would never hear of . . . one that is not known in court circles . . . and . . . like its owner—hard to find.

Prince. But now that I've found you . . . You'll never be hard to find again. I've waited all my life to find you and now . . . I'm never going to lose you.

No. 13.   *Duet* " Single-hearted "
Prince and Cinderella.

3

PRINCE.   (*Sings.*)
> I knew no sweetheart's charms
> I knew no lover's arms
> Passionate words ne'er impelled me
> No amorous glance ever held me
> For you I've waited long
> To sing to you this song.

Refrain.

PRINCE.   }
CINDERS.   }
> Single hearted—fancy free
> Hoping one day that you'd fall for me
> Keeping faith—being true
> To a dream lover—I didn't know who
> Now I've found you, nothing's wrong
> My heart is singing love's old sweet song
> Kisses to music—heart beats the rhyme
> Yours to eternity—yours for all time.

CINDERS.
> I've known no happiness,
> I've known no fond caress
> Life has been sombre and dreary
> My heart has been empty and weary
> For you I've waited long
> To sing to you this song

2nd Refrain.

(PRINCE *and* CINDERS *sing.*)

(*As the refrain ends they remain embraced.*)

CINDERS.   Oh, I'm so happy.   It seems like a dream and I'm afraid I shall awaken at any moment.

PRINCE.   It is a dream but it's a dream that will last forever.   A dream of happiness that will come true in the sharing of it . . . my sweetheart.

CINDERS.   My dream lover.

(*They kiss.   The* BARONESS *enters R., sees the lovers and makes to withdraw but changes her mind after some hesitation.   Then she comes forward.   CINDERS) sees her and is afraid that the* BARONESS *will recognise her.*)

Oh . . . someone is coming . . . Lady Hangover
. . . I must go ! (*She tries to release herself but the*
PRINCE *holds her fast.*)

PRINCE. No, no. Stay with me, my darling.
(CINDERS *struggles and breaks away. She runs off L.,*
but turns to blow a kiss at the exit.)

BARONESS (*archly*). Oh dear, Prince, do forgive me.
I had no idea I was intruding . . . she seemed a very
pretty girl . . . who is she ?

PRINCE (*sulkily*). I don't know . . . but I'm going
to find out. (*Towards L. exit.*)

BARONESS. Stay a minute . . . I have an idea I've
seen her somewhere before.

PRINCE (*turns eagerly*). Yes ? . . . Yes. She
seemed to know you.

BARONESS. Now wait a minute. Where was it ?
. . . Epsom . . . No . . . The Riviera ? . . . No
. . . Switzerland ? . . . No . . . Paris ? . . . No
. . . Billingsgate . . or—er—Billingsgate was the
town house of my first husband . . . but . . . No
. . . I've got it ! . . . She must have been one of my
regular customers—er—er—I mean—er—clients . . .
you know, the guests at my bridge parties every third
Thursday. You should come along one afternoon,
Prince. We have such fun and even if you don't play,
my two little girls will always keep you amused . . .
but for the life of me I can't remember anything
about her.

PRINCE. Then you don't know who she is ?

BARONESS. Oh yes. I know her very well, but
I just can't call her name to mind . . . but my two
little girls will know. I'll call them.

PRINCE (*hastily*). Oh no, I beg of you.

BARONESS. No trouble at all, Prince ! (*Calls.*)
Hortense ! Ermyntrude ! Hortense ! Ermyntrude !
. . . Drat the girls. Why don't they answer. I'll
have to go and find them. . . . I won't be a moment.
(*Giggles and exits R.*)
(*The* PRINCE *exits hastily almost upsetting* BUTTONS
who enters L.)

PRINCE. Ah, Richard, my good fellow. Do you know where my beautiful lady is ?

BUTTONS. Yes, sire. In the rose garden.

PRINCE. Then keep that old beldame and her two ugly ducklings away from the rose garden for the next hour or so.

BUTTONS. Must I ?

PRINCE (*laughing*). Just to show your devotion !

BUTTONS. Sir—I will do even that—for you !

(*The* PRINCE *exits L.*)

(*And* BUTTONS *grins.*) Who'd be a Prince . . . in love ?

(BARONESS *and the* TWO DAUGHTERS *enter.*)

ERMYN. 'Ow, you've been telling fibs, our mum. The Prince ain't here !

BUTTONS. His Royal Highness, madam, begged me tender you his apologies. He has been called away for a short time on urgent business.

BARONESS. There now ! . . . Oh well, never mind. We'll see him later.

HORTENSE (*sidling up to* BUTTONS). Will you dance with me, Lord Stoneleigh ?

ERMYN. No, 'e won't. 'E's going to dance with me, ain't yer ?

BARONESS. Children, children, you forget yourselves. . . . Lord Stoneleigh, I should like to dance.

ERMYN. } O-o-o-oh !
HORTENSE. }

BUTTONS. I'd like to oblige you all but I can't dance with three at once. Suppose we play games.

ERMYN. } How lovely ! Yes ! Yes ! Very
HORTENSE. } delaightful !
BARONESS. }

BUTTONS (*up C.*). Right. Then I'll go and hide and you count up to fifty and then come after me and the one that catches me, I pay a forfeit to. Is that all right ?

ALL. Yes   (*They run across to L.*)

BUTTONS.   Then off I go.   Hide your faces and no cheating.

(THEY *hide their faces*.)

(BUTTONS *exits rapidly up C.*)

(*The others count.   The* BARON *enters, sees them, turns to go up C. back as counting ends.   They see him and mistake him for* BUTTONS.   THEY *shriek with delight and chase him round the stage.   He breaks into a run, around L. and then up C.*)

ALL.   After him !   There he is !   I've nearly got him !   (*Ad lib.*)

(THEY *all exit up C.*)

(BUTTONS *enters R. calmly but suddenly the hue and cry is on, the others run in L. and* BUTTONS *is soon also involved as quarry and red herring.   However, it is the* BARON *who is eventually run to earth and collapses on the ground with three women on top, all demanding forfeits, as* BUTTONS *escapes up C.*)

BARONESS.   Daughters !   Daughters !   Get up this minute !   How can I claim the forfeit with you smothering poor Lord Stoneleigh ?

ERMYN.   } (*As they draw away*.)   But I caught
HORTENSE. }   him—I saw him first !

BARONESS.   Not another word . . . I caught him . . . and I'm going to claim the forfeit. . . . Come along, Lord Stoneleigh, don't be bashful. . . . You're going to enjoy this as much as I am.   (*Bus.*)

BARON (*taking hands from face*).   Am I, darling ?

(*Collapse and* BLACK OUT.)

CURTAIN.

During Scene change:

(*In front of tabs, enter the* SISTERS.   *They go into*:—)
No. 14. Duet . . .
                HORTENSE AND ERMYNTRUDE

Act II.

Scene 3.

Scene.—*The Ante-Room.* (*As in Scene* 1.)

(*When the Curtain rises on stage are:*—Cinderella, Prince, Baron, Baroness, Buttons, The Fairy Godmother, Hortense, *and* Ermyntrude.)
(*They dance a minuet*).

No. 15. *Dance* (*Minuet*)   ...   Principals

(*At a given moment before the end of the dance there is heard the deep booming chimes of midnight.* Prince *and* Cinderella *are at* C., *and* Cinderella *stops dancing. They all stop, and watch, surprised. The* Prince *goes up to her, but she wards him off with her hands. He checks.*)
Prince.   My lady . . . !

Cinders (*as the chimes go on*).   No—no—*no* !

(*She turns, and runs up the steps and off* R. *along the rostrum, leaving her glass slipper.*)

Prince.   After her, Richard !   After her !

(*They dash up the steps and look off* R. *and* L., *and exit running.*)

Baron.   What extraordinary behaviour !
Hortense.   I wonder what she's up to !
Ermyn.   Forgot the back door key, I suppose !
Baroness.   I wonder where I've seen her before.
Baron.   Come, wife, daughters.   The Prince is distraught.   We must leave.
Hortense.   But it isn't over yet.
Ermyn.   The dancing isn't finished, is it ?

(*The* Baron *shepherds them off* R. *They exit, except* Baron, *as* Buttons *re-enters* L.)

Buttons.   Ah, Hangover, the Prince wants you to help me find the mysterious lady.

BARON. I will be with you as soon as I have informed my wife—ahem ! *if* I can find her !

(*Exit R.*)

BUTTONS. I hope to goodness she and her two brats don't want to come too . . .

(PRINCE *enters,*)

ah, sire . . . What fortune ?

PRINCE. I cannot see her anywhere. . . . Does Hangover go with you ?

BUTTONS. He does, Your Highness.

*PRINCE (*sitting L.C.*). Tell them to put out the lights, Richard, and go. Spare no pains to find her—scour the town and countryside but bring her back to me . . . for I love her dearly.

BUTTONS. You—*love* her ?

PRINCE. Yes—yes—yes !

BUTTONS. In other words—yes ! Good-night, my Prince.

(*Exits R.*)

(*The lighting changes to moonlight. The music of the refrain of " Single-hearted " is heard softly and the* PRINCE *begins to sing it, dejectedly as the curtain falls slowly.*)

CURTAIN.

* *SPECIAL NOTE.—If, for convenience, this scene is played in the Palace Garden, instead of the Ante-Room, the first sentence of the Prince's speech is altered to:—*

Hurry, Richard, hurry ! Do not waste a moment ! Spare no pains . . . (*Etc., as above.*)

ACT III.

SCENE 1.

SCENE.—*A Road to the Baron's House.*

(*The curtain rises as the entr'acte dies away.*)

(*Enter the* BARON *L., somewhat inebriated but maintaining an exaggerated decorum and precision of speech. He moves with dignity to C.*)

BARON (*bowing to an imaginary Prince*). Your Royal Highness ! I deeply regret to state, to report, to divulge, that, after an extensive investigation and microscopic examination of the purlieus of the metropolis not omitting the (*local*) Housing Estate, I have been unable to elicit, educe, unearth, disinter or otherwise discover the slightest trace, vestige, indication, mark or sniff of the whereabouts of the lady whose acquaintance you desire to resus—resus—resuscitate ! . . . In other words—I can't find her. Thanking you one and all for a very pleasant evening. . . . (*Looks off R.*)

But stay ! Here come a further bevy of nymphs, among whom may be the filly in question !

(*Very softly, the orchestra plays a quick-step, as various ladies of the chorus enter R., and cross over quickly to L., and off. As the* BARON *addresses each of them, they pass him without checking, and merely throw a line at him, or none at all:*)

BARON.	Excuse me . . .
1st Lady.	No thank you . .
BARON.	Excuse me . . .
2nd Lady.	I haven't the time . . .
BARON.	Excuse me.
3rd Lady.	I bought a flag yesterday
BARON.	Excuse me . . .
4th Lady.	I'm a stranger about here . . .

BARON.   Excuse me . . .
5th Lady.   I shall give you in charge . . .
BARON.   Excuse me . . .
6th Lady.   I haven't any change . .
BARON.   Excuse me . . .
7th Lady.   You could work if you wanted . . .
BARON.   Excuse me . . .
8th Lady.   Granted !

(*When the last lady has gone off R., the* BARON *is left
    exhausted. He wipes his brow, comes down stage and
    says to the audience*:)
BARON.   Excuse ME . . .

(*He goes into*:—)

No. 16. *Song*   ...   .   BARON.

(*After Number*:—*Enter* BUTTONS *L., wearing a long
    cloak and hat. The* BARON *thinks he is a lady.*)

BARON.   Excuse me . . . (BUTTONS *throws off his
cloak.*) Well ! For Scotland Yard !

BUTTONS.   Have you found her ?

BARON.   Have I found her ! I've very nearly been
arrested. I've been looking for you, too, all over the
place.

BUTTONS.   Did you find me ?

BARON.   Not a sign of you anywhere . . . you'd
better come and help me look.

BUTTONS.   But what about the lady ?

BARON.   Not a sausage—I've been to every vicinity
in the pub.

BUTTONS.   I believe you ! I think I'll see you home
and then report to the Prince.

BARON.   Don't want to go home.

BUTTONS.   You'll catch it from your wife if you
don't.

BARON.   I'll catch it from her if I do ! I'll tell you
something, Stoneleigh old boy . . . I hate that
woman, and I loathe her daughters. But I'll have my
revenge ! D'you know what ?

BUTTONS.   No—what ?

BARON. I'm going to—to—sew up the legs of their pyjamas !

BUTTONS. Oh, you couldn't do that old boy ! Think of the old School ! Floreat Etona and all that tripe !

BARON (*much moved*). Shades of my Alma Mater ! How could I think of such a caddish trick !

BUTTONS. What were you, old man ? Oxford ?

BARON. No—Cantab, old boy, Cantab. Where were you ?

BUTTONS. Oh, Borstal, of course.

BARON. Stout feller ! When did you come down ?

BUTTONS. You don't go up and down at Borstal, you go in and out.

BARON. Quite ! Quite ! A splendid tradition! Ah, happy days, happy days ! I love to reminisce about the old place !

BUTTONS. Where were you born ?

BARON. Chorlton-cum-Hardy. Where were you ?

BUTTONS. Oh, somewhere around at the time ! Look out ! A lady !

BARON (*turning to R.*). Splendid ! This may be she—her—she ! Watch me, old boy . . .
(*A Lady, heavily cloaked has entered R., and moves to C.*)

BARON (*approaching with a courtly air*). Excuse me . . .

LADY (*revealing herself*). EGBERT ! (*It is the* BARONESS).

BARON.
BUTTONS. } (*together*). Excuse ME !

(BLACK OUT.)

CURTAIN.

Act III.

Scene 2.

Scene.—*The Baron's Kitchen.*

(*The* Baroness *is seated at the R. end, and the* Sisters *above the table.* Cinderella *is serving the* Baroness *with porridge.*)

Baroness.   Take it away ! Take it away ! (Cinderella *takes the porridge towards L.*)

Ermyn.   Oy ! Where you taking that there
porridge ? I want some more.

Cinders (*returning*). I'm sorry.

Hortense.   More porridge ?

Ermyn.   Yes, more porridge ! Any objection ?

Hortense.   I don't know where you put it.

Baroness.   Don't be vulgar. (*Drinks tea out of her
saucer.*)

Hortense.   No more do I, after all that supper she
had last night at the Ball.

Ermyn.   Supper ? I only had ten sandwiches,
nine sausage rolls, eleven cream buns and 'arf a dozen
bottles of that there lemonade.

Baroness.   That's enough, now !

Hortense.   Half a dozen ? Quite disgusting !

Ermyn.   It was lovely ! Quart bottles all done up
in silver paper, in ice buckets.

Hortense.   Silver paper ! Ice buckets !

Baroness.   Ermyn*trude* ! That wasn't lemonade—
it was champagne ?

Ermyn.   It might have been skin lotion—it was
still lovely ! I brought a bottle 'ome for the mornin' !

Baroness.   You never did !

Hortense.   Quaite revolting ! Behaving like a
gutter-snipe !

ERMYN. Gutter-snipe yourself! Coo! What a pity you wasn't at the Ball, Cinders! You would have enjoyed it—ever so!

HORTENSE. Ay hardly think she'd have appreciated the atmospheah!

ERMYN. (*nudging* HORTENSE). You never saw such dresses, Cinders—ooh! wasn't they daring!

HORTENSE. Definiteleh blush-making!

CINDERS. Did you dance with the Prince?

BARONESS. Did they dance with the Prince! He danced with practically no one else—the first part of the evening!

ERMYN. *and*⎫ (*After exchanging glances*). Yes, the
HORTENSE. ⎬ first part of the evening!

BARONESS. Until that rather common girl in the white dress and glass slippers come in and simply threw 'erself at the Prince as you might say.

ERMYN. Oh, she wasn't so bad to look at!

HORTENSE. Not may stayle! Too much goo-goo baby blue eyes!

BARONESS. I thought it very bad form the way she be'aved. As for the Prince, if it'd been anyone else it'd have been just bad manners. (*Licking the jam spoon.*) Still, it never come to nothink!

CINDERS. Why—what happened?

BARONESS. We was all dancing and everythink very pleasant except for my bunions, when the clock struck twelve and she 'opped it.

HORTENSE. *H*opped it, mother.

BARONESS. I mean what I said—she buzzed orf.

CINDERS. But why?

BARONESS. Search me.

HORTENSE. Some kitchen maid on her night out, if you ask me.

ERMYN. Gate-crashing—the bold 'ussy!

BARONESS. But the funny thing *h*is—I seemed to have seen 'er somewhere—as I told the Prince.

CINDERS. You told the Prince? (*She stifles laughter and runs off L., as* HORTENSE *replies:*)

HORTENSE. And why shouldn't she? Impudence!

BARONESS. Oh, we had a very confidential chat, the Prince and me.

ERMYN. Go on, Mum ! What did 'e say ?

BARONESS. Never you mind—'cept that I put in a word for you both.

HORTENSE. You never ! Well, I didn't have that, but I—er—I had a very naice taime !

ERMYN. Yerse ! I saw yer !

BARONESS. Saw her where ?

HORTENSE. Oh, shut up, our Ermyntrude !

ERMYN. Yes I did ! Down the bottom of the garden behind the currant bush !

HORTENSE. Currant bush ! It was the rhodeo-dedendrons !

BARONESS. Well, currants or rhubarb—what was his name ? What was 'e like for 'Eavens sake ?

HORTENSE (*bashfully*). Oh, ever so nice ! Lovely curly hair and blue eyes, and beautiful clothes and a scented hankie !

BARONESS. Did he—did he kiss you ?

HORTENSE (*giggling coyly*). Yes, ma !

BARONESS. Are you going to see him again ? Tell mother !

HORTENSE. He's going to take me to the Rex next Thursday.

BARONESS. Good girl ! You've played your cards very well—that'll learn you, Ermyntrude.

ERMYN. Don't you worry—I've got all my cards still in the pack !

BARONESS. Yes, and there they'll stay if you ask me ! (*To* HORTENSE.) What was his name ?

HORTENSE. I don't know !

ERMYN. (*like a child*). I know 'is name, ma ! I know 'is name, ma !

BARONESS (*to* HORTENSE.) Why didn't you ask ?

HORTENSE. The Prince come along and he had to go.

BARONESS. Why ?

ERMYN. I can tell you !

BARONESS *and* HORTENSE. Who ?

ERMYN. Ha ! Ha !
HORTENSE.   Don't be a cat ! }
BARONESS.   Who is he ?   } (*together.*)

ERMYN.   He's the Prince's . . . (*goes into a fit of laughter*).

BARONESS *and* HORTENSE.   Yes ?

ERMYN. . . . Second footman !

(BARONESS *and* HORTENSE *go into hysterics.*)

BARONESS (*rising and going down R.,* HORTENSE *following*).   Go away from me—go away ! (*Pushes* HORTENSE *away to C.*)   What daughters !   After all I've done for you—after sacrificing myself and marrying that old bag of bones just to give you a chance in Society and everythink that money could buy so as you could get an 'usband at the Ball—and what 'appens ?   One of you swipes the Palace champagne and the other goes canoodling in the cauliflowers with a footman !   You're no better than that old stop-out Hangover !   Ten o'clock and he's still out—looking for the Prince's mysterious lady—I see him !—going up to all the girls in the High Street !   And me sitting at home (*Collapses on bench.*) all forlorn and woe-begone and neither comfort nor joy to ease me poor old bleeding heart. (*Sobs. The* SISTERS *set up a loud howl.*)

(*The sound of a trumpet is heard off R., and the* BARON *enters, flushed and happy with his trumpet. His clothes are in disarray, and he waves his walking stick like a sword. The others back, rather scared to L.C.*)

BARON.   Hail. . . .
BARONESS.   You'll get no hale 'ere, you drunken . . .

BARON.   HAIL ! (*Waves his stick with a flourish.*)
HORTENSE.   He's mad !
ERMYN.   He's barmy !
BARON.   Hail to thee, Blithe Spirits !

ERMYN. Spirits !

BARON. HAIL !

BARONESS. Don't you hail me, you—slubberde-gullion, you sink of iniquity. . . .

BARON. Aha ! Aha ! (*Approaches them, menacing-ly. They retreat as he advances, and they back up L., across upstage to R., and down R. as he comes after them*)

Aha ! What's this ? The slut is shrewish ! Hold thy peace, hussy, or I will make thee a gag of one of thine own fishcakes . . .

(*He vaults over the table, crashing into the crockery, and lands on the bench. They all scream and crouch down R.*)

ALL. Help ! Police ! Murder !

BARON (*rising*). Silence, beldames ! Or I will have ye cast into my deepest dungeons, there to plague and torment the rats. Rats ! Grey rats—blue rats—pink rats. . . .

(CINDERELLA *runs in L.*)

CINDERELLA. Daddy ! Daddy ! What's the matter ? Aren't you well ?

BARON (*bowing*). I am in excellent health ! (*As the others move.*) Down, rabble ! (*Turning back to* CINDERELLA.) Don't I look well ?

CINDERELLA. Yes, daddy ! But where have you been—and where is poor Buttons ?

BARON. Ha ! Button me no Buttons ! For the Buttons ye thought were Buttons are no longer Buttons—(*confidentially*) not even hooks and eyes ! He is . . . (*pauses*)

BARONESS. Oh, can't no one do nothink ?

BARON. He is . . . *Lord Stoneleigh* !

ERMYN. ⎫ Ow gracious !

HORTENSE. ⎭ Mummy !

BARONESS. He's mad as well as drunk !

BARON. Lord Stoneleigh ! (*Flourishes trumpet and stick.*)

BARONESS. Cinders ! Do somethink ! Get him
off to bed !

CINDERELLA. Come along to bed, Daddy—you've
been up all night—you must be tired.

BARON. True—true—I am a trifled fatigued . . .
(*Moves to her at L. C. The others relax and move—
he swings round.*) Back, scullions ! (*To* CINDERELLA.)
Your arm, dear lady ! (*as* CINDERELLA *takes him out
L.*) I would fain recline upon a bossy mank—a massy
bonk—a bonky mass . . . (*yawns*)—heigh-ho !

(*They exit L.*)

BARONESS (*coming C.*). There you are ! That's
married life !

HORTENSE. I thought we were all going to be
murdered !

ERMYN. I feel as if I 'ave been !

BARONESS. Never mind, my daughters ! At least
we've been guests at the Palace—and whatever little
blunders we may have made—there's always good fish
in the sea !

SISTERS (*disgusted*). Fish !

(*They go into:—*)

No. 17.   *Trio* ...
            BARONESS, HORTENSE, ERMYNTRUDE.

After Number (*and dance if desired*):—

FANFARE *of* TRUMPETS *off.*

(*Enter* CINDERELLA *L., in great excitement.*)

CINDERELLA. The Prince ! The Prince !

BARONESS. The Prince ? Don't be silly ! What—
blowing bugles in the street ?

CINDERELLA. No ! That was the Court Trum-
peter. The Prince is sitting in his carriage, while
Lord Stoneleigh—Buttons—calls at the houses with a
box.

ERMYN. With a box ?

HORTENSE. What's he collecting for ?

CINDERELLA.   I don't know. . . .

(*Enter* BUTTONS, *R.   He carries a glass slipper in a casket.   The others are C., and L.C.   He comes down to R.C.*)

BUTTONS.   Your servant, ladies.   (*Bows low.*)

ERMYN.   Not 'arf you ain't !

BARONESS.   Where've you been to ?

BUTTONS.   On the Prince's service.   (*Holds up the casket.*)   In this casket lies a glass slipper, worn last night by the beautiful lady with whom the Prince has fallen in love.   As you know, she left the Palace hurriedly, and the slipper fell from her foot as she ran away.   The Prince, in ignorance of her name and residence, has decreed that whichever lady this slipper fits—and perfectly—shall be his bride. . . .

(BARONESS *and* SISTERS *rush at him.*)

One at a time, ladies, one at a time, ladies !   I don't suppose the slipper will fit any of you three. . . .

BARONESS.   How dare you . . .⎫
HORTENSE.   You see if it doesn't . . . ⎬ (*together*)
ERMYN.   What a nerve . . .⎭

BUTTONS (*airily*).   Well, well !   We can but try— we can but try !   Be seated, please.   (*They all sit on the bench below the table.*   CINDERELLA *retreats to stool down L.*)

(*to* BARONESS.)   This will hardly interest you—as you're already married !

BARONESS.   Won't it though !   (*She tries on the slipper as* HORTENSE *hops down R. on one foot trying to get her shoe off, and* ERMYN *goes L. and sticks out her foot for* CINDERS *to pull her shoe off.*)

BUTTONS (*after a struggle*).   Really, madam, you must admit that you're forty years too late . . . next lady please !

BARONESS.   Let me tell you . . .

BUTTONS.   Next lady !   The Prince will grow impatient !   (*As* HORTENSE *sits on the bench.*) . . . good Heavens !   (*Views her foot.*)

HORTENSE.   Now Mumsy, your ickle Horty's going
to try !   I'm sure it'll fit !

ERMYN.   You might get it on your big toe—*with* a
struggle !

HORTENSE.   Pig !   (*Bus. with* ERMYN *and* BARONESS
bandaging foot, adjusting bunion pads, etc., as HORTENSE
tries.)
Oh, try again—again !   (*She tries again—pushes and
pushes—eventually kicks* BUTTONS *over on his back.*)

BUTTONS.   This is a shoe fitting, not a Soccer
Match !

(HORTENSE *goes into hysterics and drums her heels on
the ground.*   BARONESS *takes her up* R. *and tries to
pacify her as:*)

ERMYN. (*coming to bench*).   Now for it !   Smack
it on, boy !   Half a mo' !   (*Pulls off a few inches of
stocking.*   BUTTONS *seizes it, and pulls yards of stocking
off.   If possible, heavy metal garter comes away with top
of stocking and falls with a clang.*)

HORTENSE (*breaking away and coming to* BUTTONS).
I want another try !

BUTTONS (*handing her the garter*).   Consolation
prize.

(HORTENSE *smacks* ERMYN, *who kicks her, and she
collides with the* BARONESS.   BUTTONS *prepares to
fit shoe, very exasperated.*)

BUTTONS.   For the last time of asking !

(*The fitting is a terrible struggle of a tug-of-war kind,
ending with* ERMYN *falling off the bench and* BUTTONS
falling back on the others.   CINDERELLA, *who has
watched all this is highly amused.*)

ERMYN.   Ow, it's not fair— and I did want to be a
Princess !

(BUTTONS *picks himself up and goes* L.C.)

HORTENSE.   It's a fraud !   No grown girl could
wear a slipper that size !

(*The* SISTERS *sit on the bench and wail.*)

BARONESS.   Never mind, daughters !   be brave !
We've done our best !

BUTTONS. Yes, and nearly killed me into the bargain !

BARONESS. You get out ! We don't want you 'ere ! Come to make game of us !

BUTTONS. I'll go the moment my task is done !

BARONESS. It is done !

BUTTONS. Oh, no ! The Prince commands that *every* lady must be tried. You three have failed. . . .

ALL. Well ?

BUTTONS. But what about our little Cinders, here ?

BARONESS. What ! The serving wench ? Never ! I won't 'ave it !

ERMYN. Wot ? 'Er ? (*Goes into raucous laughter with* HORTENSE, *they both slap each other on the back as they roar with laughter.* ERMYN *falls off the bench.*)

BARONESS. She shan't ! She shan't !

BUTTONS. Wench ! The Baron's daughter ! And every lady must be tried—the Prince's orders, ma'am !

BARONESS. Orders ? She's not to try, d'ye hear ? And who gives orders in this house, I'd like to know ?

(BARON *enters* L., *with a handkerchief round his head.*)

BARON (*L.C.*). I DO ! And what's this hullabaloo ? Well, Stoneleigh ?

BUTTONS. The Prince's orders, sir. The mysterious lady at the Ball left this glass slipper, and whoe'er it fits will be his bride. And every lady's bound to try.

BARON. Don't tell me it fits one of those—those—(*gulps*) one of those ? Unless it's a horse-shoe !

BUTTONS. I've tried them all without success—except for Cinders here, and now the Baroness *insists* she shall not try !

BARON. Insists ! Against the Prince's strict command ? It's treason ! (*To* CINDERELLA.) Sit down, dear child, and try the slipper on. (*The* SISTERS *retreat to* R.C.)

(CINDERELLA *sits on the bench. The slipper is fitted on.* BUTTONS *leaps up.*)

BUTTONS. It fits ! It fits ! (*Rushing to R.*) Out of my way—for I must tell the Prince ! (*Exit R.*)

BARON. I'm not surprised !

ERMYN. The Prince will be when he sees what he's got !

HORTENSE. As if he'd marry her !

BARONESS. It's all a plot !

(BUTTONS *re-enters R.*)

BUTTONS. His Royal Highness, Prince Charming !

(*Enter the* PRINCE. *He comes down C.* CINDERELLA *stands L.C. the* BARON *at L., below her.*)

PRINCE (*as he comes in*). Where is she—where is she ?

BUTTONS (*at R.C., sweeping* BARONESS *and* SISTERS *down R.*). This is the lady, sir.

PRINCE. Her ! (*Staggered.*) But no !

(CINDERELLA'S *face drops. She retreats to the* BARON.) We must search further for the maid I love !

(*Enter the* FAIRY GODMOTHER *L. She comes to L.C.*)

FAIRY GODMOTHER. Continue your search no further, Prince. It ends here !

PRINCE. Who are you, woman ?

FAIRY GODMOTHER. Never mind who I am . . . but mind one thing, and mind it well.

PRINCE. What do you mean ?

F. GODMO. Your Princely word, my lord. The oath you swore to wed the maid the slipper fitted. (*To* CINDERELLA.) Come here, my girl. Can you match the slipper ?

CINDERELLA. Indeed I can, dear godmother.

F. GODMO. Then go—and do so. (CINDERELLA *hesitates.*) At my command !

(*Exit* CINDERELLA *L.*)

The slipper fits—the maid must be your bride, unless you wish to be for ever branded craven.

BUTTONS. Your Highness—that is true.

BARONESS. Don't do it, Prince !

BARON. Peace, wretched creature !

ERMYN.   Ow, it's a shame !   A kitchen wench to be a Princess after all !

HORTENSE.   It doesn't matter what you swore !

F. GODMO.   An oath's an oath—a Prince's oath is doubly so !

PRINCE.   That's very true.   It doesn't matter now. The slipper fits—so small—so dainty I thought that only one in all this land could wear it.   Just one ! As peerless as the stars—her beauty like the dawn— and so I gave my word—and I will keep it.

F. GODMO.   Oh, wisely chosen, Prince—for see !

(CINDERELLA *re-enters L., dressed as she was for the Ball.   She comes to C.*)

What say you now ?

PRINCE (*turning to see* CINDERELLA).   It's my lady— my love—my darling bride !   (*They embrace.*)

BARON.   My daughter.

HORTENSE.   Oh now we're for it !   He'll chop our heads off, every one !

(BARONESS *and the* SISTERS *fall on their knees wailing for mercy.*)

PRINCE.   What shall we do with them, sweetheart ! I have some dungeons, dark and damp, with rats and bats and toads and snails.   (*The others wail.*)   It is for you to say !

CINDERELLA.   No, I am so happy—everyone else must be happy too.   And I forgive them anything they did to me.

PRINCE (*to the others*).   Then rise, and thank your Princess for the mercy shown.   Baron, you shall be an Officer of State, with fifty thousand crowns a year. (*To the others.*)   Behave yourselves in future, ladies, and one thing more . . .

BARONESS *and* SISTERS.   Yes, your Highness ?

PRINCE.   Don't be late for the wedding tomorrow— I would have you there !

(*The others are relieved and delighted.*)

And one thing more ! (*pause*).   The Fairy Godmother must be there—to whom we owe this happiness.

CINDERELLA. Of course ! She must be there !

(*She runs and kisses the* FAIRY GODMOTHER *and the* BARON *and then runs back to the* PRINCE *as they all come down for the finale:—*)

No. 18.   *Finale* ...   ...   FULL COMPANY.

ALL.	Cinderella ! Cinderella !
	Happy be your wedding day
	Sunny all your morrows
	Charming then in every way
	Banish grief and sorrows.
BARON.	I wish you every happiness
BARONESS.	I humbly beg your pardon (*curtsey*)
BUTTONS.	The Cinder wench is your Princess
PRINCE.	They've truly learned their lesson.
HORTENSE.	I was a mean and spiteful cat
F. GODMO.	I hope you will regret it.
ERMYN.	And I was just as bad as that
CINDERELLA.	And now we'll all forget it !

(CHORUS *enter R. and L. up stage.*)

ALL.	Happy be your wedding day
	Sunny all your morrows
	Charming then in every way
	Banish grief and sorrows.
	Cinderella ! Cinderella !

CURTAIN.

FURNITURE AND PROPERTY PLOT.

ACT I.

SCENE 1.
    Table. (C.)
        Chairs—2 above, 1 at each end.
        Bench below table.
        Stool at hearth.
        Bench (or cupboard). (R.)
    Pot of porridge boiling at hearth.
    Four sets of plates, porridge bowls, spoons, etc., at
        table.
    Ladle for porridge. (*For* CINDERELLA.)
    Letter with Royal seal. (*Off stage* (O.P. *for*
        BUTTONS).)
    Clock Chime. *Off stage* (P.S.).
    Pail and scrubbing brush. (*For* CINDERELLA. *On
        stage* (*near fire-place*).)
    Broom. (*At R., for* BUTTONS.)

SCENE 2.
    Trumpet. (*For* BARON.)
    Lemon. Dice. (*For* BUTTONS.)
    Clock chime. *Off stage* (P.S.).

SCENE 3.
    Strike all breakfast things from table.
    Feather duster on table. Two mirrors strutted on
        mantel.
    Trumpet in case. (*For* BUTTONS.)
    Parcels with frocks, hats (in boxes) as required by
        producer. (*For* SISTERS.)
    Trick doll's house (on wheels if preferred). *Off
        stage* (O.P.).
    Pumpkin. Rat trap. *Off stage* (O.P.)
    Sedan chair. *Off stage* (O.P.).
    Ball dress fitted on spring. Wig and head dress
        (*For* CINDERELLA.) *Off stage* (P.S.).
        Wand. Glass slippers hidden in dress. (*For*
        FAIRY GODMOTHER.)
    Flashbox for final B.O. (*Effect.*)

Act II.

Scene 1.
  Rostrum and steps (see ground plan).
  Seat at L.C.
  A lute on, or near seat.

Scene 2.
  Rostrum and steps as for Scene 1.
  Garden seat L.C.

Scene 3. No props.

Act III.

Scene 1. No props. (During interval Baroness has changed into Act III, Sc. 2 dress, covered by long cloak.)

Scene 2.
  Breakfast props as for Act I, Scene 1.
  Trumpet. Walking stick. (*For* Baron.)
  Glass slipper (on velvet cushion) in casket. (*For* Buttons.)
  Long trick stockings. (See note on iron garter.) (*For* Ermyntrude.)
  Large handkerchief (*for* Baron's *head*). *Off stage* (*P.S.*).
  Glass slipper. (*For* Cinderella.) *Off stage* (*P.S.*).
  Fanfare of Trumpets. (*Effect. Off stage O.P.*)

EFFECTS:

The only " magical effects " are:

(1) The doll's house. This can usually be made locally, or hired from a firm specialising in conjurors' apparatus. It should be large enough to contain the actress playing the Fairy Godmother. The house has two " fronts." The outer one, when opened, reveals a " false " front just behind it, painted so that it *looks* as if it is well back in the " house." This false front can be in the form of two pieces, hinged at the sides exactly as the outer front is hinged, and is opened *with* the real front on the *second* occasion, by the Fairy Godmother. A much simpler way is to make the " false " front a roller blind which is raised by the Fairy Godmother *after* the house is closed (when Buttons exits for the furniture) so that when the real front is again opened, the Godmother is revealed. The main interior of the house should be painted dead black.

(2) Cinderella's transformation. Underneath her ragged dress which she wears in Act I, is the " front " of her " Ball dress " which is pinned up so that it does not show. The remainder of her Ball dress is just off stage (P.S.) and is fitted on a spring, and put on from the back in one movement. Cinderella exits in the " black-out " (P.S.) and slips off her rags, allowing the front of her Ball dress to fall into position. At the same time, her dresser fits on the Ball dress from the back. The wig and head-dress is in one piece and takes only a moment to put on. Stockings need not be worn as the dress will be full length.

During the " black-out," while this change is made, and during the Godmother's " incantation " the two footmen enter (O.P.) with the sedan chair. Careful rehearsal for timing is needed to ensure that Cinderella and the footmen are " on " before the lights go up once more.

There are no other properties which need to be made specially. The very long stocking (with heavy iron garter) is, of course, a very simple matter.

One might mention, however, that if your " Baron " cannot play the trumpet, this must be played in the wings by a musician, who will follow the Baron's " business " closely.

COSTUMES:

These are more or less traditional, and can be hired. Those for the Ball Scenes are of the " powder " period. The incongruities caused by any departure from " period " by the Ugly Sisters in the Kitchen Scenes are permissible, and add to the fun.

MUSICAL NUMBERS:

In this pantomime several lyrics have been provided. You will probably find someone on the musical side of the production who can set these to attractive melodies, but they need not be used. If " published " numbers are employed they should be chosen (so far as the Ball Scenes are concerned) with some special care, so that the charming and romantic atmosphere of the scenes is not spoiled. They should be essentially English, and have honest sentiment rather than false " sentimentality." " Jazz " numbers should not be inserted in these scenes. Those published herein should be retained if at all possible.

LIGHTING:

No very elaborate effects are called for, but spot lighting from the " perches " and/or the front of the house should be arranged if possible. Your electrician must see that it is possible to get a " black out " without difficulty (including the fire spot), and he should provide a dimmer because on several occasions the fading in and out of light is desirable, though not, of course, absolutely essential. If no " spotting " is possible (although in these days it can almost always be hired locally), at least try to secure a good stage flood on the sky-cloth. Alternatively, see that the batten on the cloth is augmented by a good " ground row " of lamps behind the rostrum so that all shadows are " killed " on the cloth.

LIGHTING PLOT.

ACT I.

SCENE 1.

(*If opening chorus is sung in front of tabs.*)
Floats blue, $\frac{1}{4}$. Colour wheel on chorus for Number
Black out at end of Number. CURTAIN UP.

(*If Opening Chorus sung off stage:—*)
Floats amber, pink, blue, $\frac{1}{2}$, during Number, and
fade to black out at end of Number. CURTAIN UP.

As curtain rises:—Fade in fire glow, orange and red.
At the same time, fade in floats, blue only to $\frac{1}{2}$.
Follow slowly with floats and battens all circuits
to full *except white* which stops at $\frac{1}{2}$.

(NOTE.—*This cue should be completed while*
CINDERELLA *hums refrain.* (Or CHORUS *sings 2nd
half of Number.*) CLOCK STRIKES *immediately cue
is complete.*)

Amber lengths on interior backing.
Perches spot for numbers as desired.

CUE. *As* BUTTONS *and* CINDERELLA *sing the last
two or three lines of first refrain:*—Fade out all
lighting except spots from perches. Curtain falls.
Spots on principals as they sing 2nd refrain in
front of tabs. (Augment with floats and No. 1
batten, amber and pink, if needed.)

SCENE 2.

To open: Floats and No. 1 batten amber, pink, blue
$\frac{3}{4}$, white $\frac{1}{4}$,—centre sections only.
Perch floods C. acting area, straw.

CUE. BUTTONS. "A lemon!": BLACK OUT

During Scene change: Lighting as for Scene 2, for
Number 5.

SCENE 3.

To open: Lighting as for Scene 1, ON for curtain
rise.

For No 6: O.P. perch No. 7 pink frost on CIN-
DERELLA.

For No. 7: Perches spot SISTERS straw and white
frost.

For No. 8: Perches spot CINDERELLA No. 4 amber and No. 7 pink. Check whites to ¼.

CUE 1. BUTTONS *exits for furniture*: Quick fade-out of white in floats and battens and check other circuits to ¾. Perches straw and pink on C. acting area.

CUE 2. F. GODMOTHER: *On 2nd* " Close your eyes " ! BLACK OUT (*including fire*).

CUE 3. F. GODMOTHER: " Take this lady to the BALL." *Immediately on* " BALL ": *Lighting* UP.

CUE 4. F. GODMOTHER: " On my broomstick ": (BLACK OUT. CURTAIN.)

ACT II.

SCENE 1.

To open: Floats and battens, amber, pink, blue, full. White ½ (*C Section only.*)

Stage flood and ground row on cloth, No. 32 blue. Perches flood stage acting area No. 7 pink and straw.

(*Perches out at end of opening chorus.*)

For No 10: Perches focus spot on PRINCE No. 7 pink and straw.

For No. 11: Perches flood stage as for No. 9.

(*Ditto for No. 11a.*)

SCENE 2.

To open: Floats and all battens (except batten over cloth) pink and blue full. Amber ½. White ¼. Stage flood, batten, and ground row on cloth, blue full. (*Change stage flood if possible to No.* 20 *blue.*)

For No. 12: Perches flood stage No. 10 pink and No. 18 blue.

(*Focus perches on* CINDERELLA *and* PRINCE *as the company. dances off, changing pink to No. 7 for Number*) (*Fade perches at end of Number.*)

CUE. BARON: " Am I, darling? ": BLACK OUT.

During Scene change: Floats and battens full up Perches spot sisters for Number, No. 7 and straw.

SCENE 3.

    To open: As for Scene 1.

        NOTE.—*If this scene is played on Scene 2 set, lighting is as for opening of Scene 2.*)

    Perches flood stage No. 7 pink and No. 16 blue (or 18).

    CUE. CHIMES: Focus perches on CINDERELLA. Follow her up steps. OFF *as she exits.*

    CUE. *Exit* BARON, BARONESS *and* SISTERS: Commence check of all amber in floats and battens to NIL. Pink to ½.

    Change stage flood on cloth to No. 20 blue.

    P.S. perch fades in on PRINCE, No. 10 pink, and follows him to seat L.C. O.P. perch fades in on PRINCE for Number, No. 18 blue.

    Immediately BUTTONS is off stage, take out pink in floats and battens quickly and check blues to ¼.

ACT III.

SCENE 1.

    To open: Floats and No. 1 batten, blue and pink, ½. Perches spot C. of stage No. 18 blue and No. 10 pink.

    CUE. *As* BARONESS *reveals herself, and* BARON *shouts*: " Excuse me ! ":—BLACK OUT.

SCENE 2.

    Lighting as for Act I, Scene 3.

    For No. 18 (*Finale*): Perches flood stage pink and straw.

MADE AND PRINTED IN GREAT BRITAIN BY
BUTLER & TANNER LTD., FROME AND LONDON